THE MODAL BOOK

One-Word Modals	Meaning (Unit Number, Page Number)
Can	Ability (Unit 1, Page 1) Permission ...*question* (Unit 5, Page 34) Request ...*question* (Unit 6, Page 44) Invitation ...*question* (Unit 7, Page 52)
Can't	Negative Ability (Unit 1, Page 1) Prohibition (Unit 3, Page 16) Probability: Inference (Unit 11, Page 90)
Could	Past Ability (Unit 1, Page 1) Request ...*question* (Unit 6, Page 44) Invitation ...*question* (Unit 7, Page 52) Possibility (Unit 10, Page 79) Indirect Speech (Unit 13, Page 109)
Couldn't	Probability: Negative Inference (Unit 11, Page 90)
Should	Advisability/Recommendation (Unit 2, Page 9) Probability: Expectation (Unit 11, Page 90)
May	Permission ...*question* (Unit 5, Page 34) Possibility (Unit 10, Page 79)
Might	Possibility (Unit 10, Page 79) Indirect Speech (Unit 13, Page 109)
Must	Obligation (Unit 4, Page 25) Probability: Inference (Unit 11, page 90)
Mustn't	Prohibition (Unit 3, Page 16)
Shall	Invitation (Unit 7, Page 52) Future (Unit 9, Page 71)
Would	Request ...*question* (Unit 6, Page 44) Invitation ...*question* (Unit 7, Page 52) Habitual Past Actions (Unit 12, Page 99) Indirect Speech (Unit 13, Page 109) Conditionals (Unit 14, Page 113)
Will	Request ...*question* (Unit 6, Page 44) Future (Unit 9, Page 71)

Phrasal Modals	Meaning (Unit Number, Page Number)
Phrasal Modals are also called "two-word" or "three-word" Modals, depending on the number of words a modal has.	
Be able to	Ability (Unit 1, Page 1)
Be about to	Future (Unit 9, Page 71)
Be going to	Future (Unit 9, Page 71)
Be supposed to	Obligation (Unit 4, Page 25)
Be to	Obligation (Unit 4, Page 25)
Be willing to	Volunteering (Unit 9, Page 71)
Ought to	Advisability/Recommendation (Unit 2, Page 9) Probability/Expectation (Unit 11, Page 90)
Had better (not)	Advisability/Recommendation (Unit 2, Page 9)
Might want to	Advisability/Recommendation (Unit 2, Page 9)
Have to	Obligation (Unit 4, Page 25) Probability: Inference (Unit 11, Page 90)
Not have to	No Obligation (Unit 4, Page 25)
Have got to	Obligation (Unit 4, Page 25)
Need to	Obligation (Unit 4, Page 25)
Not need to	No Obligation (Unit 4, Page 25)
Would like (to)	Desire & Preference (Unit 8, Page 60)
Would prefer	Desire & Preference (Unit 8, Page 60)
Would rather	Desire & Preference (Unit 8, Page 60)
Would sooner	Desire & Preference (Unit 8, Page 60)
Would (you) like...?	Invitation ...*question* (Unit 7, Page 52)
Would (you) mind...?	Request ...*question* (Unit 6, Page 44)
Used to	Habitual Past Actions (Unit 12, Page 99)

THE
MODAL
BOOK

Around the World
with
Joe and Lisa
in

EGYPT ⊰ ECUADOR ⊰ THAILAND ⊰ JAPAN ⊰ BRAZIL ⊰ FRANCE
UNITED ARAB EMIRATES ⊰ MALAYSIA ⊰ CHINA ⊰ INDIA
MEXICO ⊰ GERMANY ⊰ TURKEY ⊰ ITALY

Joseph Krupp and Lisa Tenuta

PRO LINGUA  ASSOCIATES

Pro Lingua Associates, Publishers
P.O.Box 1348
Brattleboro, Vermont 05302 USA
Office: 802 257 7779
Orders: 800 366 4775
Fax: 802 257 5117
E-mail: orders@ProLinguaAssociates.com
Web Store. www. ProLinguaAssociates.com
SAN: 216-0579

At Pro Lingua
our objective is to foster an approach
to learning and teaching that we call
interplay, *the **inter**action of language*
learners and teachers with their materials,
with the language and culture,
and with each other in active, creative
*and productive **play**.*

This book was designed by Arthur A. Burrows. It was set in Palatino and FC-Kristi. Palatino, the most widely used, and pirated, face of the twentieth century was designed by Hermann Zapf in 1948 in Frankfurt. Although modern, it is based on Renaissance designs typical of the Palatinate area in Germany. Kristi simulates hand printing and is reasonably easy to read. The illustration on page 60 is by Mark Nadel. The clipart illustrating the rest of the book is from Art Explosion 750,000 Images; Copyright © 1995-2000 Nova Development Corporation. The book was printed and bound by Capital City Press in Montpelier, Vermont.

Printed in the United States of America
First printing 2002. 3000 copies.

Contents

Introduction

The Purpose of This Book

This book is for students of English who have a high beginning proficiency level and above. The main purpose of this book is to increase your understanding of modal verbs and your ability to use them appropriately. Each unit introduces one <u>meaning</u> of modal verbs, for example: Ability, Advisability, Obligation, Request, etc. By the end of this book, you will understand the differences in meanings of modal verbs and you will be able to recognize and use modal verbs in your own reading, writing and speaking.

How to Use This Book

This book can be used either in class with a teacher or as a self-study text. The answers to the exercises are in the back of the book.

Each unit has the same basic parts. They are described below.

Explanations

The explanations are in boxes. They show you the modal verbs and their meanings. There is also information about how to make questions and negative sentences. In each box, there are examples of the modal verbs in sentences.

In some of the units, there are "Be careful!" warnings because you might confuse the meaning of one modal with another. Read each of the boxes in the beginning of the units very carefully, so that you will understand the forms and meanings of modal verbs.

Exercises

The next part of the unit is a series of exercises. Usually, there are 5–7 exercises in each unit. The first few exercises are easier than the later exercises, which are more difficult. If you have questions while you are doing the exercises, look back at the boxes in the beginning of the units.

Readings

The final part of each unit is a reading that uses the modal verbs that are introduced in that unit. These readings are designed to help you better understand how modals are used and to give you more practice using them. Some of the readings have comprehension questions. Some of the readings have tasks for you to do after you do the reading.

What are Modal Verbs?

Modal verbs are words that modify the meaning of sentences in English. Perhaps the easiest way to see how modal verbs work is to look at what happens when we add modals to sentences.

Sentence with no Modal	Meaning
*Jack **traveled** around the world last year.*	This tells you what Jack did. It's a fact.

Sentences with Modal Verbs	Meaning
*Jack **couldn't travel** around the world*	This means that Jack did not have the **ability** to travel or there was a **prohibition** against it.
*Jack **had to travel** around the world last year.*	This means that there was was an **obligation** for Jack to travel. It was necessary.
*Jack **may have traveled** around the world last year.*	This means that you are not sure what Jack did. It tells you about a **possibility.**

Questions Often Heard about Modals

Do I have to know the meanings and uses of all of the modals? There are so many.

No, you don't. Our advice is for you to know the usual meanings and use one or two modals for each meaning. Over time, as your language skills increase, you can begin to use more modals in a number of different situations.

How do I know if this "can" is ability, request, permission or invitation?

This happens often with modals. You see the same modal with a number of different meanings. Look at the **One-Word and Phrasal Modal** charts that give the forms and meanings of modals. They are at the beginning of the book on pages ii and iii. The main way to understand the meaning of a modal verb is by its context. Ask yourself these questions: "What is the speaker or the writer trying to say? What is the situation?" These questions will help you understand the context.

Do I have to use modals?

No, you don't. You can avoid using modals. However, if you use them, you will speak more like a native speaker, and, in many cases, you will be able to say more in fewer words.

Look at this example:

It's possible that I will go out to dinner with my mother tonight.	Six words
Maybe I will go out to dinner with my mother tonight.	Three words
I may go out to dinner with my mother tonight.	Two words

As you can see from these examples, in the sentence using "may," you say the same thing but with fewer words. Sometimes, when you're learning a language and you are afraid of making mistakes, you should try to keep things simple. We hope that this book will make modal verbs easier for you and that you will enjoy learning more about them.

J.K. and L.T.

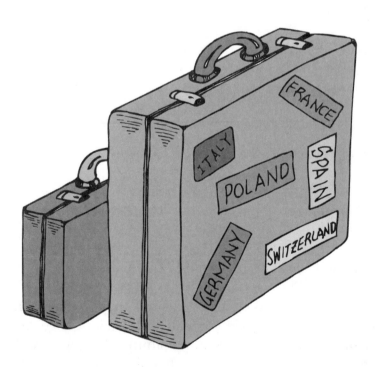

A Trip to Egypt

Can, Be able to
→ Use these to express an ability that a person has. This ability may be natural or acquired, or mental or physical.

1.1 *From our hotel room, we can see many colorful feluccas on the Nile.*

1.2 *If Mark wants to ride a camel, he can ride one at the Pyramids.*

1.3 *Our tour guide, Ahmed, is able to drink five cups of tea in an hour and go to sleep afterward.*

Future: Can & Will be able to
→ Use *will be able to* for all future abilities.
→ Don't use *can* when the future ability is learned or acquired.

1.4 *After I study Arabic, I'll be able to read and write better.* (This is a learned or acquired ability.)

1.5 *We can go shopping in Port Said next week.* (This ability is <u>not</u> learned or acquired.)

Past: Could & Was/were able to
→ Use these to express past abilities.

1.6 *We couldn't get too close to the Sphinx because it's being repaired.*

1.7 *Wagdi was able to go to Alexandria to visit his family.*

> *Be Careful: Negative Ability vs. Prohibition*
> ✈ Don't confuse negative Modals of Ability with Modals of Prohibition.
> See Unit 2 for Modals of Prohibition.

1.8 *You can't take pictures in the Egyptian Museum.* (It's prohibited by law.)
1.9 *I can't take pictures of Old Cairo today.* (I left my camera on the tour bus.)

> *Related Expression: Know how to*
> ✈ Use this to express an **acquired ability** only. Most of the time it refers to a skill
> you have. A skill is something you learn by practicing.

1.10 *Do you know how to say "Thank you" in Arabic?*
1.11 *I don't know how to get to the Khan el-Khalili. People say it's a great place to shop.*
1.12 *Maha and Shahira didn't know how to snorkel before they went to Hurghada.*

Exercises

Exercise A. Read the conversation. Underline all the Modals of Ability and any Related Expressions.

The Friend Who Can't

Farida: Let's go out and do something. I'm tired of staying inside all day.

Ahmed: You're right. Let's go for a swim.

Farida: I can't. I don't know how to swim.

Ahmed: That's OK. Do you want to go for a bike ride?

Farida: I can't ride a bike, either.

Ahmed: Really? I didn't know that. How about a movie, then?

Farida: I'd love to, but I can't see without my glasses. I left them at school.

Ahmed: Oh, that's too bad. *(Thinks.)* I know! We can play some music. I know how to play the
guitar, and you can sing with me.

Farida: Maybe you'll able to play, but I certainly won't be able to sing.

Ahmed: Oh, come on. I know you sing really well.

Farida: OK, I'll sing. But you have to sing with me.

Ahmed: All right, but don't laugh at me when you hear how terrible I sound. I really can't sing at all.

Write all the things Farida and Ahmed can and can't do.

Exercise B. Write three sentences about what each person can or is able to do.

1. A musician

   A musician can read music.

   _____

   _____

2. A doctor

   _____

   _____

   _____

3. A mother

   _____

   _____

   _____

4. A tour guide

   _____

   _____

   _____

5. A police officer

   _____

   _____

   _____

6. A taxi driver

   _____

   _____

   _____

Exercise C. Write five things you can and can't do in the chart below. After you finish, write five sentences about things a friend or a classmate can and can't do.

CAN

CAN'T

_____   _____

_____   _____

_____   _____

_____   _____

_____   _____

_____   _____

Exercise D. Use <u>could</u> and <u>was/were able to</u> and fill in the blanks in these conversations. Use the appropriate positive, negative, or question forms. Some conversations have more than one correct answer.

1. **Mother and Daughter**

   Mother: Did you see the doctor today?

   Daughter: No, I _____ get in. She was too busy, but I can see her next week.

2. **Boss and Employee**

   Boss: _____ find the information I wanted?

   Employee: No, I wasn't. I'll try again tomorrow.

3. **Two Co-workers**

   Co-worker 1: I _____ come to work yesterday because of the snow.

   Co-worker 2: Oh, I _____ because my new truck never has any problems in the snow.

4. **Two Friends**

   Friend 1: Hi. I haven't seen you in a long time. Did you have a nice vacation?

   Friend 2: No, I never went. I _____ get time off from work. And, I _____ afford it, anyway.

5. **Daughter and Father**

   Daughter: What did you do to my new car?

   Father: Well, it was raining really hard. I _____ see and I _____ stop in time.
               Before I knew what was happening, I hit a tree.

   Daughter: Oh no! How can I get to work tomorrow?

6. **Two Sisters**

   Sister 1: What do you think you're doing? That's my new sweater.

   Sister 2: I _____ find mine, so I just borrowed yours.

   Sister 1: Sorry, but I'm wearing it tonight.

Exercise E. Use Past Modals of Ability to write a question and a positive and negative response for each statement.

1. **I can speak French.**

   <u>Could you speak French (five years ago)?</u> (Question)

   <u>Yes, I could speak it, but not very well.</u> (Positive)

   <u>No, I couldn't speak it at all.</u> (Negative)

2. **My friend is able to run very fast.**

   _____ (Question)

   _____ (Positive)

   _____ (Negative)

3. **Metwally and Omar can play the piano well.**

   _____ (Question)

   _____ (Positive)

   _____ (Negative)

4. **Khalid knows how to do many things on the computer.**

   _____ (Question)

   _____ (Positive)

   _____ (Negative)

5. **Rafik is able to travel to many countries.**

   _____ (Question)

   _____ (Positive)

   _____ (Negative)

Exercise F. Use Past Modals of Ability to write three short conversations. Use the conversations in Exercises D and E to help you.

_____

_____

_____

_____

_____

_____

_____

_____

Exercise G. Read the sentences with Future Modals of Ability. Underline the modals that are <u>not</u> correct and rewrite them with the correct forms.

1. Next year, I can speak Arabic very well.

2. Next year, I can return and visit the Pyramids in Egypt.

3. Alia can play the piano very well in two years if she practices every day.

4. Mustafa will be able to go with us next week, but not tonight.

5. I can belly dance after I finish this dance class.

6. I can take pictures in the Egyptian Museum if I remember to bring my camera.

7. You can eat cheap and delicious food around Tahrir Square in Cairo.

8. You can drive like a professional after you take the driving course next month.

9. Farida can swim after school if the pool is open.

10. Ali can paint better pictures if he works harder.

Exercise H. Imagine that you were alive in 1900. What could and couldn't you do? Write 5 sentences.

1. _I couldn't drive a car._ _____

2. _____

3. _____

4. _____

5. _____

Imagine that you will be alive in 250I. What will you be able to do? What won't you be able to do? Write 5 sentences.

1. _I'll be able to see my friend when we talk on the phone._

2. _____

3. _____

4. _____

5. _____

Exercise I. Read the story. After you read, underline all the Modals of Ability and Related Expressions. Then answer the questions.

The Old Man and His Magical Powers

There is a small village in the northern mountains where a strange and mysterious old man lives. From the village, I can see his dark wooden house way up in the mountains, but I never see him at all.

People say he's strange and mysterious because he can do magical things. They say he can make things appear and disappear at any time. He can become invisible and walk through the village streets at night, and no one is able to see him. He knows how to grow beautiful flowers outside in the winter time. I once saw lovely red roses blooming in front of his house even though the ground was covered with snow. Some people say that he can talk to wild animals. Others claim that he can understand what the animals say to him. Maybe the animals are the only real friends he has.

I'm surprised to hear of all the mysterious and magical things he can do. But I often wonder how he is able to stay alive without going to the village to buy food and other supplies.

Many villagers ask, "How can he live that way? How is he able to survive the long years and hard winters alone?"

How can I answer them? I can't. I can only continue looking for him and hoping that one day I'll be able to meet him and ask him these questions myself.

Questions: What do you think about the old man?

1. Where does the old man get his special powers?
2. How is he able to survive without going to the village?
3. Do you know any stories about people who can do strange and mysterious things?
4. If you could have any one magical power, what would you like to be able to do?

More Practice

Write the story in the Past. Make all the necessary changes.   *(Answers on page 117)*

A Trip to Ecuador

Can't, Mustn't

➔ Use these to express something that is prohibited by a rule, a law or a situation. **Can** is used more than **must**, especially in informal language.

➔ These can also be written as **must not** and **cannot**, but the contractions are usually used. When you use **must not** and **cannot**, you can stress the not for more emphasis.

2.1 *You can't climb that volcano. It's a restricted area.*

2.2 *We can't take any plants from the national park. It's prohibited.*

2.3 *You mustn't go off the footpaths on the Galapagos Islands.*

2.4 *I'm sorry, Bob can**not** keep that Spanish book overnight. Mr. Fierro needs it.*
(Emphasis on <u>not</u>.)

2.5 *Please tell them they must <u>not</u> take photos in the Guayasamín Museum.*
(Emphasis on <u>not</u>.)

Related Expressions: be not allowed to, be not permitted to, be forbidden to

➔ Use these to express something that is prohibited by a rule or a law.

➔ Write the verb "be" in the past, present or future, depending on the time.

2.6 *We weren't allowed to wear shorts in the baths at Baños. We had to rent bathing suits.*

2.7 *Because of bad weather, our plane won't be permitted to land at Quito's airport.*

2.8 *Smoking is forbidden inside the San Francisco church.*

Exercises

Exercise A. Rewrite each phrase using must not/mustn't or cannot/can't.

1. Smoke on domestic flights in the U.S.

   You mustn't (can't) smoke on domestic flights in the U.S.

2. Wear short pants in that new restaurant.

3. Take a photograph in the Egyptian Museum without a permit.

4. Park next to a fire hydrant.

5. Throw garbage out of your car window.

6. Eat with your left hand in the Middle East and India.

7. Wear shoes inside your Japanese friend's house.

8. Cut down trees in a national forest.

Exercise B. Write three things that you mustn't do in each of the following places.
Use Modals of Prohibition and/or Related Expressions.

1. at the airport

   a. _____

   b. _____

   c. _____

2. in a hospital

   a. _____

   b. _____

   c. _____

3. at an embassy

a. _____

b. _____

c. _____

4. in a supermarket

a. _____

b. _____

c. _____

5. in an English class

a. _____

b. _____

c. _____

Exercise C. Read the conversations. Write one reason why each of the following activities is prohibited. Be sure to write a complete sentence. Begin your sentence with you and include because.

1. A: You can't swim here.

   B: Why not?

   A: *You can't swim here because the beach closes at 5 pm when the lifeguard goes off duty.*

2. A: You mustn't smoke at my mother's house.

   B: Why not?

   A:

3. A: You are not permitted to take photos here.

   B: Why not?

   A:

4. A: You can't park in this area.

   B: Why not?

   A:

5. A: You are not allowed to climb that fence.

    B: Why not?

    A:

6. A: You cannot talk in here.

    B: Why not?

    A:

Exercise D. Different countries have different rules about which activities and behaviors are
prohibited. Think of the countries you know and write a list of 10 things that are forbidden.

E   _In the U. S., people are not allowed to drink alcohol in bars or restaurants_
      if they are under 21 years old.

1. _____

_____

2. _____

_____

3. _____

_____

4. _____

_____

5. _____

_____

6. _____

_____

7. _____

_____

8. _____

_____

9. _____

_____

10. _____

_____

Galapagos Islands

Exercise E. Put the words in the sentences in the correct order.

1. dog can't here in you bring your

    <u>You can't bring your dog in here.</u>

2. in temples the mustn't shoes your wear in Thailand

    _____

3. flash cannot this in a use we museum

    _____

4. the to their use exam notes the were during forbidden students

    _____

5. young not ride bicycle street in was I when the permitted to my

    _____

6. you go after curfew out dark mustn't there because is a

    _____

7. in bar drink U.S. not a allowed the are you twenty-one old in to years are you if under

    _____

    _____

Exercise F. Read the story. After you read, underline the Modals of Prohibition and Related Expressions. Then, replace them with other Modals of Prohibition and Related Expressions.

No-Nos* at the Museum

*A No-No is a slang expression used for things that people can't do.
"That's a No-no" means "You can't do it."*

"It's 5:00, ladies and gentlemen. Time to close up the museum," said the young security guard on duty that evening. I could hear him saying all of this in another room. He was speaking Spanish. I could understand Spanish better than I could speak it.

I was just getting ready to take a photo of a ceramic pot when the guard walked into the room. The pot was beautiful. It was from a town in the south of Ecuador called Saraguro.

"You can't take photos in here," the guard said abruptly.

"Why not?" I asked in my bad Spanish. "I don't see any signs prohibiting it."

"I'm sorry, ma'am, but it's not allowed."

"That's ridiculous," I said. "I've been taking photos here all afternoon."

"You have?" He almost shouted this at me. "Photography is not permitted in this museum."

"Well," I answered, trying to keep my voice calm, "that's what you say now, but no one said anything when I was taking photographs this afternoon. I know we mustn't touch the exhibits, and we mustn't lean on the glass cases, but there are no rules about taking photos."

I felt happy because I could say this in another language. Of course, now it sounds better when I write it in English, but I was very proud of myself that afternoon.

"Come with me," he said, nervously. "We'll have to see the curator."

We walked downstairs. We went down a hallway, and he pushed open a door that said "Administrative Offices" on it.

He told me to wait while he went through another door. I could hear voices behind the door as the guard explained why he was there. After a few minutes, the door opened, and he told me to enter the office.

I went in.

A handsome young man was sitting behind the desk.

"Mrs. Napolitano," he said in English, when he saw me. "How nice it is to see you again."

"Enrique," I said. "What a pleasant surprise to see you here!"

The curator looked at the guard and said, "Jaime, you can go now. I will take care of Mrs. Napolitano." The guard looked at the curator, looked at me, and left.

After he left, the curator said to me, "So, my favorite English teacher from the university, what seems to be the problem?"

(Answers on page 118)

A Trip to Thailand

Should, Ought to, Might want to

→ These give advice or a recommendation. The results may not be bad if the advice is not taken. The listener may or may not take the advice.

→ **Should** is used more often than **ought to**.

→ **Might want to** is a "friendlier" way of giving advice or a recommendation.

2.1 *We should visit the Golden Temple. Our guidebook says it's the nicest temple in Bangkok.*

2.2 *If you eat a hot pepper, you should eat plain rice and drink a little hot tea.*

2.3 *Malee and Dao ought to take the Chao Phraya River taxi. It's a great way to see Bangkok.*

2.4 *Tom and Kanchana might want to go to Chiang Mai in the summer. It's cold in the winter.*

Had better, Had better not

→ Use these to express stronger advice or a recommendation. If the advice is not taken the result may be bad for the listener. It is almost an obligation. *(See Unit 4, Modals of Obligation and Necessity)*
Had better has no past form. Use the past form of **should** or **ought to**.

→ In informal spoken English, **had better** is often pronounced as "**better**."

2.5 *Passengers on the bus for Sukhothai had better bring something to eat. It's a long trip.*

2.6 *You'd better not wake up late if you want to get across Bangkok. The traffic is terrible.*

Past: Should have & Ought to have
- ✈ Make the past form with **should have** or **ought to have** + past participle.
- ✈ Do not use <u>had better</u> in the past.

2.7 *We **should have spent** more time at Koh Samet when we were in Thailand.*

2.8 *You **ought to have brought** more money with you. I don't have any more to lend you.*

Questions: Should
- ✈ Use **should** to make questions asking for advice. Do not use **ought to** or **had better**.

2.9 *Should I learn to speak Thai before I travel in Thailand?*

2.10 *Where should we eat if we want the best Northeastern food?*

Be Careful: Advice/Recommendation vs. Beliefs
- ✈ **Should** and **ought to** are also used to talk about beliefs or opinions.. In these cases, you are not giving someone a recommendation or advice.

2.11 *Jean should read a little about Thai culture before she goes to work in Thailand.* (Advice/Recommendation.)

2.12 *People should be sensitive to other cultures when traveling.* (Personal Belief)

Related Expression: Why don't you. . .?
- ✈ Use this as a friendly, more informal way to make recommendations and to give advice.

2.13 *Why don't you call my friend Pong when you get to Bangkok? He can show you around.*

2.14 *Why don't you meet Wipa and me at the Weekend Market for lunch on Sunday?*

Idiomatic Expression: A Must (Noun) and Must (Verb)
- ✈ Use these to tell your friends about something they should do.
- ✈ These are often used to talk about movies, restaurants and traveling.
- ✈ These are not obligations. They are strong recommendations from you about something you have seen or done.

2.15 *Ayutthaya is **a must** if you visit Thailand. We spent two days there!*

2.16 *You **must** visit Phuket. Its beaches are beautiful.* (**must** is emphasized)

Idiomatic Expression: Might as well
- ✈ Use this to make informal conclusions about something that is advisable.

2.17 *It's raining too hard. We might as well stay in the hotel this morning.*

Exercises

Exercise A. Fill in the blanks with **should, should not, ought to** or **had better**. Some questions may have more than one answer.

1. There's an English test tomorrow. You **should (ought to/had better)** study tonight.

2. Prasert's room is very dirty. He _____ clean it before his mother comes home.

3. Rashid and Yoko want to go to Koh Samet tomorrow morning. They _____ take the train because it's safer than driving. They _____ drive because there's nowhere to park.

4. It's a beautiful day. _____ we go to the temple at Nakorn Pathom ?

5. Dan and Brad are planning a trip to Thailand next year. Where _____ they go?

6. I want to see Thai dancing. We _____ buy tickets for the performance tonight.

7. Paveena doesn't want to cook dinner tonight. What _____ he do?

8. If Wanida doesn't feel well, she _____ stay at home. She _____ go to a doctor. She _____ hurry because many people have the flu and the doctor will be very busy.

Exercise B. Match the advice on the left with the consequence on the right.

1. Somchai had better not smoke in bed, or. . . (   )

2. You should try to speak more English in class, or. . . (   )

3. Neal might want to hurry, or . . . (   )

4. Miriam ought to stop smoking, or . . ( )

5. Darrell shouldn't drink so much coffee, or . . . (   )

6. You ought to get a haircut, or. . . (   )

7. Suzanne should ask more questions, or. . . (   )

8. Charoen shouldn't drive too fast, or . . . (   )

9. Why don't you go shopping? If you don't . . . (   )

10. They'd better make their reservations early, or . . . (   )

A. . . .she'll start a fire.

B. . . .your grandmother won't know you.

C. . . .she'll have an accident.

D. . . .your speaking won't improve.

E. . . .we won't have any snacks in the house for the party.

F. . . .she won't be able to run for the track team.

G. . . .his bus will leave without him.

H. . . .he won't be able to sleep.

I. . . .she won't understand what's happening.

J. . . .the flights to Los Angeles will be full.

Exercise C. Read the consequences. Write a sentence using the **past form** of a Modal of Advisability. (If you need help, look at Exercise B for hints.)

1. Our house caught fire last night. _Mom shouldn't have smoked in bed._

2. Akiko's English ability didn't improve. _____

3. Boonsong missed his bus. _____

4. Darunee couldn't play football yesterday. _____

5. They weren't able to sleep. _____

6. Thanom's grandmother didn't know him. _____

7. Chan didn't understand her teacher. _____

8. Sukanya had an accident. _____

9. We didn't have anything for dinner. _____

10. The flights to Chiang Mai were full. _____

Exercise D. A friend asks you for advice about the following things. Write a list of advice and recommendations for your friend. Use both stronger and weaker modals of advisability.

1. Your girlfriend wants to learn English.

   She should find a good teacher.

   She ought to try to speak with native speakers.

   She had better practice every day.

   She shouldn't speak her own language in class.

2. Your friend wants to get married.

   _____

   _____

   _____

   _____

3. Your friend has a stomach ache.

_____

_____

_____

_____

4. Your friends want to take a trip around the world.

_____

_____

_____

_____

5. Your friend wants to buy a new car.

_____

_____

_____

_____

6. Your friend wants to stop smoking.

_____

_____

_____

_____

Exercise E. In newspapers around the world, many people write and ask for advice for problems they have. Read the letters that were written to "Mr. Mike, the Advice Man" in a U.S. newspaper. Help Mr. Mike write a short answer to them.

Dear Mr. Mike:

    I am a female 19-year-old university student. I like someone in my history class, but he doesn't seem to notice me. My friends all tell me that I have a good personality and that I am attractive, but I can't get his attention. What should I do?

Wondering in Wisconsin

_____

_____

_____

_____

Dear Mr. Mike:

    I need your help very much. I study English at a university in the U.S. My classmates all understand the teacher. It seems that I'm the only one who doesn't understand the teacher. I didn't do very well on my mid-term exam, and many times I don't know what to do for the homework. Oh, Mr. Mike, I need your help quickly.

Lost in Laredo

_____

_____

_____

_____

Dear Mr. Mike:

Last night I got into an argument with my girlfriend about marriage. We are going to get married next year. She thinks she should continue working after we get married. I think she should stop working, because I want her to cook dinner for me and keep our house clean. What do you think?

Fighting in Phoenix

_____

_____

_____

_____

_____

Dear Mr. Mike:

I am a 34-year-old salesman. I'm single, and I make a good salary. The trouble is that I never seem to have any money. Yes, my apartment is expensive because I like to live in the city, and I drive a very nice car. I also eat in nice restaurants three or four nights a week and eat lunch at a gourmet cafe every day. Because I have to see many clients for my job, I have to dress well. I can't go to a cheap store and buy cheap clothes. Also, my credit card bills are very high. Mr. Mike, I need your help before I have spent all my money.

Shiftless in Chicago

_____

_____

_____

_____

_____

Exercise F. Read the story. After you read, find and underline all Modals of Advisability and Related Expressions.

What Should I Do?

It was raining hard when I left work at 6:00 pm. The sky was like a blanket of darkness, and there were already large pools of water on the street and sidewalk.

I was in a hurry because I had a dinner meeting with the company directors at 6:30, and the restaurant where we were going to meet was across town. I was carrying a large envelope with many papers for an important project the company was planning.

As I reached into my pocket for my car keys, the envelope slipped out of my hand and fell into a big puddle of water.

"Oh, no," I said out loud. "What should I do now?" I quickly dried off the envelope as much as I could, but the papers inside were soaked.

When I got into my car, I threw the envelope into the back seat and turned on the ignition. As I began to turn into the street, I almost hit a man and his child. They were crossing the street. The man was very upset.

"Hey, Mister, you ought to slow down," the man yelled at me. "You should go back to driving school, you *^%$#!!!"

I felt bad, but I had to get to that meeting. It was going to be one of the most important meetings of the year.

When I got to the restaurant, I couldn't find a parking place, so I parked a few blocks away. I had to walk a long way in the rain. I was very wet by the time I got there.

When I walked into the restaurant, the maître d' said, "You should use an umbrella on a night like this."

"Thanks for the advice," I said. "That's a great idea."

Across the restaurant, I saw the company table. My boss and the other company directors weren't there yet. I started walking quickly toward the table.

I was thinking about those wet papers and trying to make a good excuse when a waiter stepped out in front of me. He was carrying a full tray of food, and he nearly knocked me over.

"Why don't you watch where you're going?" he said. "You really should be more careful."

I said I was sorry and made my way to the company table. I saw my friend, Susan, and sat down next to her.

"What happened to you, David?" she asked. "You look terrible. You should have something to drink and relax a little."

"That's a great idea," I said. "But what I really should do is take a long vacation. I probably will. I dropped all the plans in a puddle, and the boss is going to kill me."

"No, she won't," said Susan. "Anyway, I was worried about the plans, too, so I made an extra copy of them."

"You're amazing, Susan. You should get a raise for this. You really saved the day."

"And you should go into the men's room and dry off. While you're there, you ought to comb your hair, too. If the boss sees you, she'll think you fell in the puddle, not the project plans."

"You're right. I ought to listen to you more often."

"Yeah, you should."

"If I did, I might be the boss myself someday."

"The boss!" Susan cried. "You should worry about keeping the job you have. And you had better hurry up, too, because the real boss just walked in the front door."

David went off to the men's room, and Susan sat there thinking and shaking her head. "That guy needs more than an umbrella," she said to herself. "He'd better get a whole new life!"

ADDITIONAL PRACTICE

Change all the modals of advisability to the past.

(Answers on page 119)

A Trip to Japan

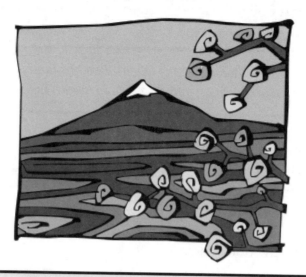

Comparing Modals of Advisability & Modals of Obligation

➔ Modals of Advisability are used to express weak or strong recommendations.

➔ Modals of Obligation are stronger than Modals of Advisability. Use Modals of Obligation for something a person is required or obliged to do because of laws, customs, rules or circumstances. There may be a penalty or consequences for not doing it.

Must, Have to, Have got to, Need to

➔ **Must** is more formal than **have to** or **have got to**.

➔ **Have to** and **have got to** are used more frequently and informally.

➔ **Need to** is a "friendlier" way of expressing necessity.

4.1 *You must take off your shoes when you go into Sachiko's house.*
4.2 *We have to meet Mr. Nomura at 10:00 tomorrow.*
4.3 *Ed has got to learn Japanese quickly if he wants to get a job in Osaka.*
4.4 *You need to go to Kyoto if you want to see Japan.*

Future: Must, Have to, Have got to, Need to

➔ Use **must, have to, have got to,** and **need to** to talk about the "near" future. *(See the examples above.)*

➔ Use **will have to** and **will need to** to talk about the "distant" future.

4.5 *Laura will have to learn to like sushi if she wants to live and study in Tokyo.*
(Distant future)

4.6 *We'll need to take the Shinkansen if we want to be in Nagoya by 9:00.* (Distant future)

Past: Had to & Needed to
→ Use **had to** for past obligation and <u>needed to</u> for past necessity.
→ Do not use **must** and **have got to**.

4.7 *I had to learn to like the public hot baths when I lived in Japan.*

4.8 *Tomoyasu needed to work late every night when he began his job at Sony.*

Questions: Have to & Have got to
→ Use **have to** and **have got to** to make questions.
→ Notice that **have got to** does not use "do" to form a question.

4.9 *Why do we have to watch sumo wrestling again? I want to watch baseball.*

4.10 *Have we got to eat horse sashimi again? We just had it last night.*
(Horse sashimi is raw horse meat.)

No Obligation: Not have to, have not got to
→ Use these when there is no obligation or necessity.

4.11 *You don't have to eat the horse sashimi if you don't think you'll like it.*

4.12 *Mark hasn't got to stay in a capsule hotel for a real Japanese experience.*

Other Expressions of Obligation: Be to, Be Supposed to
→ <u>Be to</u> is another way of expressing an Obligation and Necessity. It usually refers to a rule or a circumstance. It is not used frequently.

4.13 *Mrs. Nakamura said we are to study Ikebana for two hours a day for the next three months.* (Ikebana is the Japanese art of flower arranging.)

4.14 *You're not supposed to pass food from your chopsticks to someone else's chopsticks. You're supposed to put the food down on the other person's plate.*

Spoken English: Hafta & Gotta
→ **Have to** is usually pronounced "hafta" in informal spoken English.
→ **Have got to** is usually pronounced "gotta" in informal spoken English.
→ When "gotta" is not used, **have got to** is often contracted to **I've got to, You've got to, She's got to, We've got to**, and **They've got to**. Often, in these cases, **got** is stressed when speaking. *You've **got** to help me learn Kanji.*

4.15 We have to (hafta) wake up early to climb Mt. Fuji.

4.16 We have got to (gotta) get some of those noodles for our trip to Sapporo tomorrow.

Exercises

Exercise A. Rewrite these sentences using Modals of Obligation and Necessity.

1. Come to class on time.

   You have to (must) come to class on time.

2. Stop at all red lights.

3. Speak only English in class.

4. Chew your food well before swallowing it.

5. Watch your luggage carefully in an airport.

6. Keep your head down when you hit a golf ball.

7. Carry your passport when you are traveling.

8. Practice English outside of the classroom.

9. Listen to and respect your classmates.

10. Take the subway if you want to get around Tokyo quickly.

Exercise B. Change the sentences from present to past. Remember to make all necessary changes.

1. Megumi has to walk five miles to go to school.

    Megumi had to walk five miles to go to school.

2. Christine needs to practice speaking Japanese more .

3. Dave and Mary Sarah have got to see *Kabuki* before they leave Japan.

4. Sachiko has to report to the office tomorrow at 9 a.m.

5. Tetsuo and Akira need to get haircuts.

6. Hideo has to stay home with the children while Hiroko works.

7. Toru must exercise his shoulder every day.

8. Megumi and Hiroyuki don't have to go to bed at 10 tonight.

9. Mariko doesn't have to call home on Wednesday.

10. You need to drink a lot of water when you're climbing Mt. Fuji.

Exercise C. Read the sentences. Write three obligations and necessities for each situation. Use different modals in positive and negative forms.

1. Al's parents are coming to visit for a week.

   Al needs to go out and buy a lot of food. He also must clean his apartment, but he doesn't have to wash his windows.

2. Tomoyasu and Kiyomi are having 30 people at their house for lunch tomorrow.

3. Louise is going to Japan for a business trip.

4. David and Diane are moving to a new city.

5. Mayumi has a date on Friday night.

6. Masatoshi wants to stop smoking cigarettes.

7. John and Carolyn are going to a friend's wedding.

8. Yoko is studying to become a doctor.

Exercise D. Write the consequences for each sentence.

1. You must eat all of your dinner or _you can't have any dessert._

2. You have to eat all of your vegetables, or_____

3. Our landlord had better fix our refrigerator, or_____

4. The children have to be in by dark, or_____

5. Fumie had better not drive too fast, or_____

6. Japanese high school students must study for the exam, or_____

7. I had better call and tell them I'll be late, or_____

8. We need to be at the auditorium by 8 o'clock, or_____

Exercise E. Write the obligations or necessities for each sentence. Use **must, have to, have got to** and **need to**.

1. _You must eat all of your dinner_ , or you can't have any dessert.

2. _____ , or his teeth will continue to hurt.

3. _____ , or we won't have any food for tomorrow.

4. _____ , or she'll have another accident.

5. _____ , or you won't find a good seat.

6. _____ , or she won't be able to leave the country.

7. _____ , or his boss will be very angry.

8. _____ , or they won't have a place to live.

Exercise F. Each sentence contains one or more mistakes. Make all necessary corrections.

1. Yesterday, I must to go to the doctor.

   Yesterday, I had to go to the doctor.

2. What time had you got to be there tomorrow?

3. Do you having to study all night?

4. Yasuko didn't have to wake up early next year.

5. What was she needed to bring to the party?

6. Who have got to studying with Paul tonight?

7. Nancy don't have to meet the president next week.

8. They must to pick up their aunt at the airport on Monday.

9. You had better buying your ticket fast if you want to get a good price.

10. Does Greg and Penny have to wait here all day?

Exercise G.   Read the story. After you read, underline the Modals of Obligation and
Necessity.

The Girl Who Needed To

She was just getting out of bed when she heard a knock on the door. She looked at the clock on the wall and saw that it was already 10:00 o'clock. "Oh no!" she said. "I'm late."

She heard the knock again and this time she heard a voice, too.

"Leslie, open the door. It's me, Wendy."

Leslie quickly opened the door and noticed the look on Wendy's face.

"You're not ready yet?" said Wendy. "You must hurry up. Mr. Vernon said we have to be in class by 10:30 today. And we need to be ready for a big test."

"Oh no," said Leslie. "I forgot all about it. Come in and let's review while I'm getting ready. I have to find a clean pair of jeans to wear and I need to iron a blouse. You can talk while I'm doing it."

So Wendy talked and Leslie worked quickly to get everything prepared for her 10:30 class.

"It's 10:15," said Wendy. "We have to get going or we'll be late. You'd better forget about breakfast. You can always eat later."

"But I have to have a cup of coffee before I go, otherwise I won't be able to think straight," said Leslie.

"Okay," said Wendy, "but you've got to hurry."

At 10:20, they jumped into Wendy's car and sped off to the university. They arrived just as the professor was closing the classroom door.

"Hurry up and sit down," the professor said. "The exam is starting. You must use pencil only and you need to check your work carefully. It's a tricky test."

Leslie sat down near the door and immediately took out her pencil and eraser. Then she said to herself, "I have got to study more this semester, or I'm never going to graduate. But I won't think about that now. The first thing I've got to do is get a decent grade on this test and I'll be all right." She then reached into her backpack and took out a pair of glasses. She put them on and leaned to the left. This gave her a perfect view of the student's test in front of her. She squinted a little and thought, "The second thing I need to do is get a stronger pair of glasses."

Discussion Questions

1. What do you think about Leslie's behavior?
2. What happens in your class when someone cheats on a test?
3. What would you do if you saw someone cheating on a test?

(Answers on page 120)

A Trip to Brazil

May, Could, Can

➔ Use **May, Could**, and **Can** to ask permission from someone else in order to be able to do something. These modals use "I" and "we" in questions.

➔ To be more polite, use "may" or "could."

➔ **Please** is often used to be more polite. Note the position of "please" in the examples.

5.1 *May I call you when I get to Salvador?*

5.2 *Could I visit an English class when I come to your school in Curitiba?*

5.3 *Can we please dance on your float during Carnaval?*

Affirmative Answers

➔ **Yes, Sure**, and **OK** are some affirmative answers.

➔ Use **may**, and **can** in affirmative answers.

5.4 *May I please change my reservation for the Amazon trip?*
     Yes, you may.

5.5 *Could we use your car to visit Iguaçu Falls in the morning?*
     OK, but be careful.

5.6 *Can I borrow the keys to your hotel room, please? I want to change into my swimsuit*
     before I go to Copacabana Beach.
         Sure, you can, but don't forget to bring back my keys.

5.7 *May we please take photographs of a Yanomami village?*
    No, you can't.

5.8 *Could I reserve a place on the bus into the Amazon rain forest?*
    I'm sorry, you can't. We don't have any more room.

5.9 *Can we swim at this beach?*
    I don't think so. You have to go to another beach.

5.10 *Are we allowed to take photographs of a Yanomami village?*
5.11 *Are we allowed to have a barbecue on the beach late at night?*

Exercises

Exercise A. For each place, write three questions of permission. Use as many of the Modals of Permission as you can.

1. At your friend's house

    Can I play the piano?

    _____

    _____

2. At a hotel

    _____

    _____

    _____

3. At the airport

    _____

    _____

    _____

4. In a park

_____

_____

_____

5. In a shopping mall

_____

_____

_____

6. In a museum

_____

_____

_____

7. In a taxi

_____

_____

_____

8. At a university

_____

_____

_____

_____

_____

Exercise B. Write questions and positive and negative answers for each of the following situations. Use as many forms as you can.

1.   *At the Store.*

a) You want to pay for a pack of gum with a $100 bill.

Can I pay for this with a hundred-dollar bill? (Question)

Yes, you can. (Positive Answer)

I'm sorry, you can't. We don't have any change. (Negative Answer)

b) You want to return something.

_____ (Question)

_____ (Positive Answer)

_____ (Negative Answer)

c) You are in a hurry and want to go in front of the person ahead of you in line.

_____ (Question)

_____ (Positive Answer)

_____ (Negative Answer)

2.   *In the Library*

a) You want to take out a reference book.

_____ (Question)

_____ (Positive Answer)

_____ (Negative Answer)

b) You want to open the window for some fresh air.

_____ (Question)

_____ (Positive Answer)

_____ (Negative Answer)

c) You want to move a table and chairs so you and your friends can work together.

_____ (Question)

_____ (Positive Answer)

_____ (Negative Answer)

3.   *With the Neighbors*

a) You want to park in their driveway.

_____ (Question)

_____ (Positive Answer)

_____ (Negative Answer)

b) You want to use their pool while they're out of town.

_____ (Question)

_____ (Positive Answer)

_____ (Negative Answer)

c) You want to pick apples from the tree in their yard.

_____ (Question)

_____ (Positive Answer)

_____ (Negative Answer)

Exercise C. Write a question asking for permission for each answer.

1. A: _Can I go out with Johnny tonight, Mom?_

   B: OK, but you have to be back by 10:00.

2. A: _____

   B: Sure. You can give it back to me tomorrow.

3. A: _____

   B: Sorry. I didn't bring my wallet.

4. A: _____

   B: No. I'm wearing it tonight.

5. A: _____

   B: I'm sorry, but it's out of order.

6. A: _____

   B: All right, but don't eat too many.

7. A: _____

   B: Sorry. Someone's already sitting here.

8. A: _____

   B: No. It's too cold in here.

Exercise D. Choose the appropriate answer for each question.

1. Can we use a dictionary on tomorrow's test?
   a. Yes, but wait until Tuesday.
   b. Certainly not.
   c. Yes, they are.
   d. Maybe she will.

2. Could I borrow your car until this evening?
   a. No. He's not feeling well.
   b. Yes, that's a good idea.
   c. Sure. Let me know.
   d. OK, but be careful.

3. Are the children allowed to stay up until 11:00 on Friday night?
   a. I don't think so.
   b. Sorry, they don't remember.
   c. No, it's too far.
   d. Sure, they will.

4. Can I put my backpack here?
   a. Maybe, but when?
   b. Sorry, I don't have any.
   c. No, thanks.
   d. Yes, you can.

5. Are you allowed to go to the movies?
   a. I hope not.
   b. Yes, it's OK.
   c. No, I'm not hungry.
   d. Yes, I like it.

6. May I take a picture in here?
   a. I don't think it's allowed.
   b. Yes, you will.
   c. No, you won't.
   d. Yes, I will.

7. Can I visit you again sometime?
   a. No, it's too long.
   b. Sure, I am.
   c. Yes. When?
   d. Maybe, but they're busy.

Exercise E. Find the mistakes and correct the sentences.
  Make all of the necessary changes.

1. Is they allowed play volleyball here?

    Are they allowed to play volleyball here?
    _____

2. May I to borrow your car tonight?

    _____

3. Could we saw the exhibit now?

    _____

4. Can I goes to shopping with you?

    _____

5. Are he allowed going to the concert tomorrow?

    _____

6. May we to come to your class next weeks?

    _____

7. Can we to using your apartment for a party this weekend?

    _____

8. Could I to travel there without a visa?

    _____

Exercise F. Read the story. After you read, underline all of the Modals of Permission and Related Expressions.

The Permission Man

The year I lived in that small town was interesting for many reasons. But what I remember most about that year were the frequent visits from my neighbor, Mr. Johnson.

Mr. Johnson was a friendly old man. His wife had died many years before, so he lived alone in a large two-story house. He was a tall man with large, dark brown eyes. I think he must have been very good-looking when he was younger.

About a week after I moved into the house next door to his, on a Saturday morning, I think, Mr. Johnson came over to introduce himself and to welcome me to the neighborhood. I thought that was very kind of him.

As he was leaving my house after that first visit, he said, "Well, George, it was nice meeting you." Then he looked at my yard and said, "I see you've got some rose bushes over there. Very nice rose bushes. I love roses. May I cut one or two of them to put on my table at home?"

"Sure," I answered. "Help yourself."

He thanked me and went home to get his garden shears. A few minutes later he was back in my yard, cutting a few roses for the vase on his table. I waved at him through the kitchen window. He smiled and waved back. Then, he picked up his shears and took the roses home.

And so he began his weekly visits. Every Saturday morning at about ten o'clock I'd hear the doorbell ring. Mr. Johnson would be there on the porch, stopping by to say hello.

The second Saturday he stayed only a few minutes. As he was leaving, he said to me, "You know, George, I don't buy the newspaper anymore, but I love to read it. Can I have yours after you finish it?"

"Certainly," I replied. "You can take them when you come over on Saturday."

He thanked me and picked up the newspapers that I had by the door.

Every Saturday after that, he would come by and ask me if he could take something or borrow something or use something. Once he asked for my bicycle. Another time he asked if he could sit in my lawn chair and look at my garden. Another time he wanted a cup of sugar. Another time he wanted to use my telephone because his wasn't working.

I never minded at all because he was such a nice old man.

When I moved away at the end of the year, I think he was sad to see me go. I was sad to leave, too.

Just last week, I drove by his house to see how he was doing. I saw him outside talking to his new neighbors, a young couple. He was holding the garden shears and a newspaper.

I guess he's doing just fine.

Write a list of questions Mr. Johnson asked Daniel. Use "may" or "can."

(Answers on page 121)

A Trip to France

Comparing Modals of Permission & Modals of Request

✈ Modals of Permission use "I" and "we" in the questions.

✈ Modals of Request use "you" in the questions.

✈ Between equals, asking for permission is like making a request. *(Can I look at your book?* is almost the same as *Can you let me look at your book?)*

✈ See Modals of Permission in Unit 5.

Could, Can

✈ Use **Could** and **Can** to ask someone else to do something.

✈ **Could** is more formal.

✈ **Please** is often used to make requests more polite. Note the position of <u>please</u> in the examples.

6.1 *Could you please buy me a ticket for the Folies Bergere?*
6.2 *Can you tell me the way to Montparnasse, please?*

> *Would, Will*
> ⤳ Use **Would** and **Will** to ask someone else to do something. This is a little stronger than **Could** or **Can**.
> ⤳ Use "you" with **Would** and **Will**.
> ⤳ **Would** is more formal.
> ⤳ **Please** is often used to make the request more polite. Note the position of <u>please</u> in the examples.

6.3 *Would you please explain to me how you make pâte de foie gras again? I forgot.*
6.4 *Will you get me a cup of coffee and a croissant, please?*

> *Affirmative Answers*
> ⤳ **Yes, Sure, OK**, and **Certainly** are some affirmative answers.

> *Negative Answers*
> ⤳ **No, I'm sorry**, and **I don't think so** are some negative answers.

6.5 *Can you take me to the Louvre with you tomorrow, Jean Paul?*
> *I'm sorry, but I can't. I have to meet a group of students there.*

> *Would you mind. . .?*
> ⤳ Use **Would you mind…?** to ask someone to do something you want.
> ⤳ Use **would you mind if. . .?** to ask someone if they would object to your doing something. This is similar to asking for permission.
> ⤳ To agree, the answer is **No, I wouldn't** and to disagree, the answer is **Yes, I would.**

6.6 *Would you mind taking the train to Aix-en-Provence instead of the plane? I want to see some of the country.*
> *No, I wouldn't mind at all.*
(This means the person agrees with the request and will take the train.)

6.7 *Would you mind if I go to the Louvre alone tomorrow? You make too much noise in museums.*
> *Yes, I'd mind. I think we should go together.*
(This means the person doesn't agree with the request.)

Exercises

Exercise A . Change the commands into requests. Use as many of the forms of Modals of Request as you can.

1. Bring me another cup of cafe au lait.

_____

2. Take me to the airport tomorrow. I want to fly to Marseilles.

_____

3. Show me the best hotel in Brittany.

_____

4. Tell me where the restrooms are.

_____

5. Explain to me who built the Notre Dame Cathedral.

_____

6. Carry my bags to that hotel near the Champs d'Elysees.

_____

7. Lend me some money until I cash a traveler's check.

_____

8. Open the window because it's very stuffy in here.

_____

9. Give me a ride back to the train station because I left my backpack there.

_____

10. Write your address so I can send you a postcard from Strasbourg.

_____

Exercise B. Write questions and positive and negative answers for each of the following situations. Practice using as many forms as you can.

1.   *At the Supermarket*

a) You want the clerk to get something from the storeroom.

Can you get me more of these apples from the storeroom? (Question)

Yes, I can. (Positive Answer)

I'm sorry I can't. I'm busy now. (Negative Answer)

b) You want the cashier to give you an extra shopping bag.

_____ (Question)

_____ (Positive Answer)

_____ (Negative Answer)

c) You want someone to help you carry your groceries.

_____ (Question)

_____ (Positive Answer)

_____ (Negative Answer)

2.   *In the Library*

a) You want someone to show you how to use the computer.

_____ (Question)

_____ (Positive Answer)

_____ (Negative Answer)

b) You want the librarian to help you find a book.

_____ (Question)

_____ (Positive Answer)

_____ (Negative Answer)

c) You want the people at the next table to speak more quietly.

_____ (Question)

_____ (Positive Answer)

_____ (Negative Answer)

3. *With the Neighbors*

a) You want them to turn down their music.

_____ (Question)

_____ (Positive Answer)

_____ (Negative Answer)

b) You want them to water your plants while you're out of town.

_____ (Question)

_____ (Positive Answer)

_____ (Negative Answer)

c) You want them to help you move some furniture.

_____ (Question)

_____ (Positive Answer)

_____ (Negative Answer)

Exercise C. Write short conversations for each of the following situations. Include Modals of Request and positive and negative responses in your conversations.

1. Wife and husband in the kitchen

2. Two friends in the classroom

3. Clerk in a store and a customer

4. People at different tables in the same restaurant

5. Bank robber and bank teller

Exercise D. Match the Requests with an appropriate answer.

Request	Answer
1. Would you mind turning down the radio? ( )	a. Sure. Here you are.
2. Can you tell me what time it is? ( )	b. All right, but don't come back too late.
3. Will you bring this book back to the library for me? ( )	c. Thanks. I've been waiting for over an hour.
4. Could you come in now, Mr. Andrews? ( )	d. Not at all.
5. Would you let me use your car tonight? ( )	e. Sorry I can't come then. How about Wednesday?
6. Could you please pass the salt? ( )	f. It's 9:35.
7. Would you come back to see the doctor on Tuesday? ( )	g. OK. Put it in my backpack.

Exercise E. Read the story. After you read, underline all of the Modals of Request.

The Woman in the Restaurant

I was eating in a small café when an old woman walked in and sat at the table next to mine. Although I was reading a great article in a magazine, I couldn't help listening to her conversation with the waiter.

"Are you ready to order?" asked the waiter. He was tall and from India. He was probably a student at the university in town.

The old woman looked at him and said, "Yes. I'd like a cheese sandwich please. And would you tell the cook to put lettuce on the side?"

"Certainly."

"And could you tell the cook to use wheat bread? Eating white bread is like eating air."

"Sure."

"Oh. And could you also ask him to toast the bread for me?"

"OK."

"And another thing. Could he put just a little mustard on the bread. The last time I had a cheese sandwich it was mostly mustard."

"I'll make sure to tell him, ma'am. Would you like anything to drink?"

"Yes. Would you bring me a glass of water now— two ice cubes please— and a cup of coffee with the sandwich?"

"Certainly. I'll be right back with your water." He walked back to the kitchen to put the woman's order in.

The woman looked up quickly as if she'd suddenly remembered something. She caught my eye and smiled at me. I saw the waiter come back into the dining area. He came over to her table.

"Would you like something else, ma'am?"

"Yes, please. Can you make my sandwich with Swiss cheese? I forgot to mention it before."

"I'm sorry, ma'am. We don't have any Swiss."

"How about cheddar. Could you make the sandwich with cheddar?"

"Why certainly! I'll go tell the cook."

Five minutes later the waiter returned with the woman's sandwich and a cup of coffee. For some reason, however, she didn't begin eating. She just sat there sipping her coffee, looking around the restaurant, and smiling. The waiter must have noticed this, too, because he returned to the table.

"Is there anything wrong, ma'am?" he asked.

"No, not at all," the woman answered. "I'm sorry to bother you, but could you wrap this sandwich up for me? I don't feel like eating just now."

"I'll be glad to." He left and took the sandwich with him.

When he returned, he gave the woman a bag with the sandwich.

"You've been very kind," she said. "Thank you."

I had just finished my lunch and the magazine article. I got up to pay the cashier and waited while the woman looked for the money in her purse.

I heard her say to the cashier, "Would you mind giving this to that nice waiter? He was so kind and helpful."

I looked at the bill and saw that it was a $100. The cashier noticed it, too.

"I think you made a mistake," she said to the old woman. "This is a $100 bill."

"Oh, no. There's no mistake," answered the woman. "That's exactly what that nice young man deserves." She smiled sweetly and walked out the door.

The cashier looked at me and raised her eyebrows. "Maybe I ought to think about being a waiter again," she said.

"Me, too," I said, as I turned and walked out the door.

(Answers on page 122)

A Trip to the United Arab Emirates

Invitations

→ An invitation is like a request. You want someone to do something. The difference is that you want the person to do something **with** you, not **for** you.

Invitation Forms

→ Would you...   more formal
→ Would you like to...
→ Could you...
→ Do you want to...
→ Can you...   less formal

Special Note: Shall we . . .

Use **shall we** to ask someone to go someplace or to do something with you. You are almost sure that the answer will be **yes**.

7.1 *Shall we visit the Gold Souk in Dubai tonight?*
        OK. That sounds like a good idea.

7.2   *Would you come to the Corniche with us after work?*
          Sure, I'd love to.

7.3   *Would you like to go to Sharjah Souk with us tomorrow?*
          I'd like to, but I can't. My sister is coming to town.

7.4   *Would you like to go camping in the desert at Fossil Valley this weekend?*
          Sure. That would be a lot of fun.

7.5   *Could you drive with us to Hatta next week?*
          No, I can't. I'm busy. I have a lot of work to do.

7.6   *Shall we go to the Cultural Foundation in Abu Dhabi? There's a movie tonight.*
          Yes, that's a great idea.

7.7   *Do you want to go windsurfing with us next Thursday?*
          OK. That sounds like fun.

7.8   *Can you watch the sunset with us on the beach in Ras Al-Khaimah?*
          That would be great. I'm free at five.

Related Expression: Do you want to . . .

Use **Do you want to . . .** for invitation. It is usually informal, but it can also be used in more formal situations.

7.9   *Do you want to watch the camel races next weekend?*
          Sure. I haven't seen camel racing before.

7.10 *Do you want to come to my house and eat traditional Emirati food?*
          That sounds like a great idea.

Exercises

Exercise A. Write three different questions using Modals of Invitation for the following situations.

1. You want a classmate to study with you tonight.

   _____

   _____

   _____

2. You want a friend to visit you over the weekend.

   _____

   _____

3. You want someone to have dinner with you at the new Lebanese restaurant.

   _____

   _____

4. You want a co-worker to go to a concert with you.

   _____

   _____

5. You want your boss to come to a party at your house.

   _____

   _____

6. You want your teacher to ride a camel with you and your classmates.

   _____

   _____

   _____

Exercise B. Read the invitations. Rewrite them to make them more polite.

1. *To Jack and Jackie—*
   We're going riding to the citadel at three. Join us.

   Raouf

   Dear Jack and Jackie,
       Would you like to join us on a ride to Dadnah? We'll leave at three.
                                                                   Raouf

2. *To Mrs. Riggs—*
   Come for dinner tomorrow night at 7:30. See you then.

   Jennifer

3. *To Bill—*
   Have lunch with me tomorrow. Let's go to that Mexican restaurant on South 4th Street.

   Blake

4. *To Abdullah and Nadia —*
   Visit us this summer. We have lots of room. The kids would love to see you.

   Lauren and Dave

5. *To Dan—*
   Come and watch me play basketball tomorrow night.

   Benny

6. *To Ranaf—*
   Let's go to a movie tonight. I want to see that new British movie.

   Nihad

Exercise C. Write an invitation using the words given. Then write a positive and negative response to the invitation.

1. Lunch/Tuesday/1:00 pm

   Would you like to have lunch with me on Tuesday at 1:00? (Question)

   Sure, I'd love to. (Positive Answer)

   No, I can't. I have a meeting all day Tuesday. (Negative Answer)

2. Khalaf's birthday party/next weekend

   _____ (Question)

   _____ (Positive Answer)

   _____ (Negative Answer)

3. A football game/Saturday/Dubai

   _____ (Question)

   _____ (Positive Answer)

   _____ (Negative Answer)

4. Dinner/ restaurant boat in Abu Dhabi/tonight/8:00 pm

   _____ (Question)

   _____ (Positive Answer)

   _____ (Negative Answer)

5. Hiking/next summer/Nepal

   _____ (Question)

   _____ (Positive Answer)

   _____ (Negative Answer)

Exercise D. Write an invitation for each answer given.

1. Q: *Would you like to have dinner at Sushi-cho with me tonight?*
_____
   A: *Sorry, but I don't like Japanese food.*

2. Q: _____
   A: *I can't. I hurt my back lifting a table yesterday.*

3. Q: _____
   A: *No, thanks. I don't like horror movies.*

4. Q: _____
   A: *Sure. Let's go now before it rains.*

5. Q: _____
   A: *OK, but I've never ridden a camel.*

6. Q: _____
   A: *I'd love to. I need to practice speaking English.*

7. Q: _____
   A: *I don't think so because I don't have any money.*

8. Q: _____
   A: *That would be great. I love classical music.*

Exercise E. Read the conversations and find all of the Modals of Invitation.

The Invitation That Didn't Work Out

(A series of telephone conversations)

Monday, May 19 at 10:00 am

Cynthia: Hello?

Betty: Hello, Cynthia. This is Betty. How are you?

Cynthia: Fine, and you?

Betty: Just fine. Listen. Would you like to come over for dinner on Friday night? Are you free?

Cynthia: Sure. What time?

Betty: Well, we'll eat at 7:00. So do you want to come around 6:00?

Cynthia: That sounds great. Can I bring something?

Betty: No, we'll have everything here, but I appreciate the offer.

Cynthia: OK. Then I'll see you Friday.

Betty: Friday at 6:00.

Cynthia: All right. Bye.

Betty: Bye-bye.

Tuesday, May 20 at 9:35 am

Cynthia: Hello?

Betty: Hi, Cynthia. It's Betty.

Cynthia: Hi, Betty. What's up?

Betty: Well, about dinner on Friday night, there's been a change in plans. Could you come over on Thursday night instead?

Cynthia: Yeah, I think so. I'm not busy or anything.

Betty: OK. How about the same time?

Cynthia: That sounds fine.

Betty: See you then.

Cynthia: Oh, thanks for calling. Bye-bye.

Betty: Bye-bye.

Wednesday, May 21 at 11:15 am

Cynthia: Hello Betty.

Betty: Hi, Cynthia. How did you know it was me?

Cynthia: I had a feeling you'd be calling.

Betty: Well, guess what? About dinner on Thursday, I'm really sorry, but
           we have to change it again. I have to work late, and there's no way
           I'll be able to make a dinner before 9:00. Do you want to come then?

Cynthia: That's OK, Betty. Why don't we just wait until some other time.

Betty: How about Saturday night then?

Cynthia: Sorry, but I already have plans.

Betty: That's too bad. I really wanted to see you.

Cynthia: Oh, well. Could we get together next week?

Betty: That sounds good. Sorry again about all the changes.

Cynthia: Don't worry about it.

Betty: How about if I call you next week.

Cynthia: All right, I'll talk to you then.

Betty: OK, bye.

Cynthia: Bye-bye.

(Answers on page 123)

A Trip to Malaysia

Would like

➤ Use this to express something you desire.

➤ **Would like . . .** is followed by a noun or an infinitive (to + simple verb).

➤ **Would** is usually contracted to **'d** in informal English, especially when **I** is the subject:
I'd like....

8.1 *Sylvie would like to visit Penang during her trip to Malaysia next month.*   (Infinitive)
8.2 *Saeed and Sahar would like souvenirs from Sarawak.*   (Noun)

Related Expression: Want
Use this to express something you desire.
Want is also followed by a noun or an infinitive.

8.3 *Sanjai wants to see the old architecture in Penang.*   (Infinitive)
8.4 *Yuen and Clarissa want Malay food for breakfast.*   (Noun)

> *Past: Would have liked*
> ➤ Use **would have liked** to talk about the past.
> ➤ It is followed by a noun or an infinitive.

8.5 *Bruce would have liked to spend more time on the East Coast of Malaysia.*   (Infinitive)
8.6 *Carrie would have liked a cup of tea with her roti chanai.*   (Noun)

> *Would rather, Would prefer to, Would sooner*
> ➤ Use these to show that someone prefers one thing to another.
> ➤ **Would** is usually contracted to **'d: I'd rather**, … This is true especially in informal spoken English.
> ➤ **Would sooner** is less formal and is used primarily in spoken English.

8.7 *Jack would rather spend a week swimming and snorkeling than a day in a big city.*
8.8 *Wattana would prefer to look at the sea than go swimming.*
8.9 *Stacy and Shigeki would sooner fly to Melacca than take an overnight bus.*

> *Past: Would have preferred*
> ➤ Use **would have preferred** to talk about the past. It is followed by a noun or infinitive.

8.10 *I would have preferred a calmer ride on the hydrofoil. I got a little sick.*   (Noun)
8.11 *Rudolf and Isolde would have preferred to stay in a 5-star hotel rather than a guest house.*   (Infinitive)

> *Past: Would rather, Would sooner*
> ➤ Make the past form by adding have + past participle.

8.12 *Les and Brad would rather have shopped in Kuala Lumpur than spend a week in the rain forest.*
8.13 *Marianne would sooner have watched the turtles at Rantau Abang than sleep all night.*

> *Wishing Someone Well: May*
> Use may to express your desire or wish for someone else.

8.14 *May you have a great trip to Malaysia.*

Exercises

Exercise A. Imagine that you are going to each of the countries listed. Write three things you would like to do.

Ecuador

1. I would like to visit the Galapagos Islands.

2. I would like to climb a volcano.

3. I would like to visit the Guayasamin Museum.

France

1. _____

2. _____

3. _____

Egypt

1. _____

2. _____

3. _____

Japan

1. _____

2. _____

3. _____

Brazil

1. _____

2. _____

3. _____

Thailand

1. _____

2. _____

3. _____

The United Arab Emirates

1. _____

2. _____

3. _____

Exercise B. Choose one sentence from Exercise A. For this sentence, write a Yes/No question and a Positive and Negative answer.

Ecuador

1. _Would you like to visit the Galapagos Islands?_

2. _Yes, I would._

3. _No, I wouldn't._

France

1. _____

2. _____

3. _____

Egypt

1. _____

2. _____

3. _____

Japan

1. _____

2. _____

3. _____

Brazil

1. _____

2. _____

3. _____

Thailand

1. _____

2. _____

3. _____

The United Arab Emirates

1. _____

2. _____

3. _____

Exercise C. Answer the questions with complete sentences.

1. Would you rather drink coffee or tea for breakfast?

   I'd rather drink tea for breakfast.

2. Would you rather watch TV or listen to the radio?

3. Would you rather study English in England or in Australia?

4. Would you rather eat chocolate or vanilla ice cream?

5. Would you prefer to eat dinner in a restaurant or take it home?

6. Would you rather go to bed early and get up early or go to bed late and get up late?

7. Would you rather travel a long distance by boat or by plane?

8. Would you prefer to live in the city or on a farm?

9. Would you prefer to spend your vacation in the mountains or at the beach?

Exercise D. For each set of words, write one question with *would rather* and one with *would prefer to.*

1. go to a restaurant/eat at home

    Would you rather go to a restaurant or eat at home?

    Would you prefer to go to a restaurant or eat at home?

2. watch a video/go to the cinema

3. go to a museum/visit an art gallery

4. drive a car/ride a bicycle

5. live in Paris/live in New York

6. go swimming/go jogging on the beach

7. study French/study Italian

Exercise E. Change the sentences from the present to the past. Don't forget to make all of the necessary changes.

1. He would rather eat in a French restaurant.

   He would rather have eaten in a French restaurant.

2. I would prefer to watch the basketball game on TV.

3. She would sooner visit Kuching and spend a week in Borneo.

4. They wouldn't like to live in Vermont during the winter.

5. Jean and George would rather stay in a hotel a little closer to downtown.

6. She wants to see as much of Malaysia as possible during her year there.

7. We'd prefer to go sightseeing in Kula Lumpur alone.

8. Sylvie would like to meet us at 7:00 instead of 8:00.

9. I'd prefer to take the Channel train to London because I hate flying.

10. We want to learn a little Malay before we go to Malaysia.

Exercise F. Read the story. After you read, underline all the Modals of Desire and Preference and the related expression, **want**.

The Spoiled Shopper

"I'm going to the supermarket now, Thomas, but you can stay here with your sister and finish your homework," said Mrs. Hall, Thomas's mother.

"No!" screamed Thomas. "I want to go with you. I don't want to stay home."

"Well, OK," said Mrs. Hall, quietly, "but you must behave like a good boy. Now put your shoes on and let's go."

They got into the car and drove 10 minutes to the nearest supermarket. Thomas loved supermarkets. He always wanted to see all of the bright colors of the different products. He was very quiet during the ride to the supermarket, but as soon as they got into the store, he began to behave differently.

"I want Cocoa Snacks for breakfast," he yelled. "Take me to the Cocoa Snacks…Now!"

"No, Thomas," his mother said, "we're not here to buy cereal. I would like to buy a few vegetables and some bananas."

"But I want Cocoa Snacks for breakfast!" Thomas screamed. "I hate oatmeal, and I hate orange juice."

"Thomas," said his mother, "just relax and come with me to the produce section."

Thomas walked behind his mother. He was a little angry about the Cocoa Snacks. Soon he saw cans of many different colors. He told himself the names of the different colors: red, blue, green, and yellow. He had learned them in school.

They reached the produce section, and Mrs. Hall asked, "Thomas, would you rather have spinach or broccoli for dinner tonight?"

Thomas looked away and pretended not to hear her. His mother put a bunch of broccoli into their cart. He was looking at the apples. Next to the apples, he saw a display of chocolate bars. Their wrappers were blue and red.

"Ma, I want some of these chocolate bars," he said. "Can we have them for dessert?"

"Thomas, you know we don't eat sweets. We'll get some fruit. Would you prefer apples or bananas?"

"I don't want apples or bananas. I want chocolate," he yelled. Other shoppers stopped what they were doing and looked at him. They also looked at his mother. She was embarrassed.

"Well, Thomas, I'd rather have bananas for dessert," his mother said as she put the bananas into the cart. "OK, Thomas, it's time to go."

"I want to play video games before we go home," Thomas said loudly. He had stopped crying, but he was still speaking too loudly. "Take me to the video games, Ma."

(Answers on page 124)

A Trip to China

The Great Wall of China

Will, Be going to — for Plans and predictions
➔ Use these to express a future time.
➔ Use either **will** or **be going to** to talk about plans or predictions for the future.
➔ However, **be going to** often refers to an immediate and definite future, and **will** for a more distant future.

9.1 *Yi-fei is going to meet us in Tiannenmen Square later today.* (Immediate, definite plans)
9.2 *Ellyra will go to Harbin to see the ice sculptures this winter.* (Plans, "going to" is OK)
9.3 *We'll fly to Beijing and meet Gianna there.* (Plans, "be going to is OK here)
9.4 Owen: *Have you ever eaten snake soup?*
    Tom: *No, but I think I'll probably try some when I visit the night market in Kowloon.* (Prediction)
9.5 *It's not going to rain tonight. The China guidebook said it never rains in November.* (Immediate, Definite Prediction)

Future Expectations with Be going to
➔ Use **be going to** to talk about expectations or plans that have been made earlier. These expectations are based on your previous knowledge or a previous plan.

9.6 *It's going to be cold in Harbin in January. Can't we go somewhere else?* (Expectation from your knowledge.)
9.7 *I'm going to walk to Tiannenmen Square after dinner.* (This plan was made before this moment of speaking)

> **Will & Be going to: Negatives and Contractions**
> ✈ **Will** and **Be going to** are often contracted. <u>**Will**</u> is contracted to **won't**.
>   See the examples.

9.8   *I'm sorry, but we won't have time to go to Xi'an.*
9.9   *I'm not going to eat snake soup. Are you crazy?*

> **Spoken English: Be going to**
> ✈ The "going to" of **be going to** is often pronounced **gonna**, but it is always
>   written **going to**.

9.10   *Gianna said she's "gonna" learn a little Chinese before her trip.*
9.11   *We're "gonna" take the train from Hong Kong to Guangzhou next Monday.*

> **"Future in the Past" : Would & Was/Were going to**
> ✈ In speaking and writing about the past time, we can still refer to future time.
>   We often do this with verbs such as *know, think, believe, feel, seem, remember,* etc.
> ✈ In this situation, use **would** and **was/were going to**. Often the event did not
>   happen, and another sentence with "but" completes the thought.

9.12   *At the time, I thought I would never come back to China, but I did..*
       (In the past, talking about the future.)
9.13   *Jill thought she would take the train from Beijing to Shanghai, but she couldn't read*
       the sign and went to Mongolia instead.
9.14   *I was going to see the Great Wall, but I ran out of money.*

> **Be About To**
> Use **be about to** to talk about an intention in the very near future, often within
> the next minute.

9.15   *Paulina and Jiang are about to leave. Let's say goodbye.*

> **Shall**
> Shall is rarely used in North American English to mean future time. It is used
> as an invitation (see Unit 7), and it is sometimes used to emphasize a very
> strong intention or prohibition.

9.16   *I know this trip will not be easy, but I shall do it, easy or not.*
9.17   *Motorists shall not leave their vehicles unattended.*

> **Willingness with Will and Be Willing To**
>
> ✈ Use **will** to talk about willingness and promises. The emphasis is not on futurity, but rather on the speaker's desire to help, contribute or volunteer. Use **be willing to** to indicate that the person or speaker is ready and able to help. Will is more certain that **be willing to**.

9.18 *John: I'm hoping to go to Xi'an to see the statues, but I don't know the way.*

9.19 *Yi-fei: I've been there a few times. I'll take you.* (A volunteered promise)

9.20 *Zhu is willing to drive us to the Great Wall tomorrow,* (Probable, not certain) *and Jiang will do it if Zhu can't.* (Certain)

Exercises

Exercise A. Rewrite the *be going to* questions and sentences with the subjects given. Remember that "be" changes according to the subject.

1. I'm going to start university next September.

   Bob is going to start university next September.

   Sheila and Ted are going to start university next September.

2. Deng is going to give Wang a ride to school tomorrow.

   You

   Phil and I

3. Nadia and Tang aren't going to leave for Hunan tomorrow.

   Wudi

   I

4. Joanne and I are going to see the Great Wall on Tuesday.

   Leslie

   Johnny and Ling

5. What are you going to do tomorrow?

   Zhu

   Lee and Meng

Exercise B. Write questions and negative sentences for each statement. Use the question words given and also use contractions where you can.

1. Jack will meet Andrea for dinner **tonight**.

    When will Jack meet Andrea for dinner? (When)
    Jack won't meet Andrea for dinner tonight. (Negative)

2. Yumiko and Hussein will remember **their class in the U.S.**

    _____ (What)
    _____ (Negative)

3. Ji will help you clean **your apartment.**

    _____ (What)
    _____ (Negative)

4. Lina and Shirley will work **in Hong Kong** after they finish school.

    _____ (Where)
    _____ (Negative)

5. My friend will finish the Chinese cooking class **in two months.**

    _____ (When)
    _____ (Negative)

6. Ting and Eng will begin their golf match **at 12 noon.**

    _____ (What time)
    _____ (Negative)

Exercise C. Make five predictions for you, two members of your family, and one of your friends for something that will happen during the next 10 years.

1. <u>I will get married in three years.</u> _____

_____

_____

_____

_____

_____

2. My _____ (family member)

_____

_____

_____

_____

_____

3. My _____ (family member)

_____

_____

_____

_____

_____

4. _____ (your friend)

_____

_____

_____

_____

_____

Exercise D. Write the meaning for the sentences: Plan, Prediction, Expectation, Immediate future, Willingness.

1. I'll clean your house for you, Mrs. Samuels.

   Meaning _____

2. I'm going to clean your house for you this afternoon, Mrs. Samuels.

   Meaning _____

3. It will rain by the end of the month. It always does at this time of the year.

   Meaning _____

4. It's going to rain tonight.

   Meaning _____

5. It's my turn. I'll pay for our dinner tonight.

   Meaning _____

6. Jack is going to pay for our dinner.

   Meaning _____

7. Ben and Gianna are about to board the plane for Beijing.

   Meaning _____

8. Ben and Gianna were going to take Chinese lessons before they travelled.

   Meaning _____

9. Learning English will be difficult, but you can do it.

   Meaning _____

10. You can learn Chinese if you are willing to work hard.

    Meaning _____

Exercise E. Complete the conversations with the appropriate form of *be going to* or *will*. Some of the conversations may have more than one correct answer.

1. *Father & Daughter*

Father: I expect you to be home at nine o'clock tonight, Katie.

Daughter: Oh, Dad! All my friends ___*will*___ laugh if I leave at nine. How about ten?

Father: I said nine, and I mean nine.

Daughter: OK, then. I '___*ll*___ be home at nine.

2. *Two Friends*

Cary: What _____ do this weekend?

Cynthia: I'm _____ go to the beach with my sister.

Cary: That sounds like fun. Can I come, too?

Cynthia   Sure, you can. But you _____ have to wake up early.
            We like to get to the beach at 6:00.

Cary: Six! That's so early. Maybe I _____ come another time. Tomorrow,

            I _____ sleep.

3. *A Policewoman and Victim at an Accident*

Policewoman: Are you hurt, sir?

Man: I think I'm OK.

Policewoman: What's your home phone number? I _____ call your family.

Man: Thanks, Officer. They _____ be worried if I'm not home by six.

Exercise F. Read the letter and underline all Modals of the Future and Willingness. Try to describe their meanings.

I'll Meet You There

Kenosha, Wisconsin
December 1

Dear Mark:

Hey, little brother! How are you doing? I got your letter yesterday, and I want to tell you about my travel plans.

I'm going to fly direct from Chicago to Hong Kong on January 5. It's a direct flight, so I'll be on that plane for about 15 hours. You know how much I love flying, too. Since I don't know anyone in Hong Kong, I won't stay overnight there. I'm not going to bring too much money, and I won't spend what little I have in Hong Kong.

From Hong Kong, I'll transfer to a direct flight to Hebei. After so many hours in the air, I won't even know I'm flying. This part of the trip is going to be easy.

Will you meet me at the airport in Hebei? I imagine there won't be too many guys from Wisconsin in the terminal, so you should be able to find me.

I'm very excited about coming to China. This will be my first trip anywhere. Speaking a few words of Chinese will be strange. I hope no one will laugh at me.

I'll bring the clothes you want. Mom says she's going to make you another sweater, so I'll probably bring that, too.

I have more room in my suitcase. Let me know if you need more things from here. I'm not going to leave for a few more weeks, so hurry up and write.

Well, I'll go now. I'll see you next month.

Hayden

(Answers on page 126)

A Trip to India

May, Might
➤ Use these to express possibility. A possibility is something that is about 50% certain.
➤ They often refer to an intention that is not definite at the time of speaking. There is very little difference in meaning between the two forms, although **may** seems a little more possible than **might**.

10.1 *Victor might go to Rajasthan when he goes to India next year.*
(He's undecided; he isn't sure about it.)
10.2 *Sudha and Sanjeev are planning to visit the Taj Mahal. Then, they may go to the temples at Khajuraho. They were talking about it yesterday.*

Could
Could as a modal of possibility often refers to an ability.

10.3 *Raveena could travel from Calcutta to Madras by train. She could also fly.*
(This is a **possibility** because Raveena has the **ability** to travel by train or plane.)

Past: Might, Could, May
➤ Make the past form with **might have**, **could have**, and **may have** + past participle.

10.4 *Dave didn't arrive on the train, so he might have spent the night in the Maharaja's palace in Udaipur.*

10.5 *Sandra and Vijay could have taken the bus instead of the taxi to Kodaikanal this morning. They said they were going, but they didn't have much money.*

10.6 *Cindy and Brock might have done too much sightseeing in Delhi yesterday. They seem tired.*

Questions

✈ Avoid using **may** or **might** in questions, although **might** is sometimes used with question word questions. **Could** is used infrequently.

✈ Note that answers to questions about plans often express possibility.

10.7 *What are you going to do tomorrow?*
I may go shopping on the Rajpath, and then I may go to the Red Fort.

10.8 *How can we get to Cochin?*
We could take a taxi and then a ferry. We could also fly.

10.9 *Where's Lal?*
He might be at the temple in Tiruchchirappalli (Trichy). He wanted to go there.

10.10 *Could he have taken the wrong train?*

Negatives: Might, Could, May

✈ Make the negative forms with not: **might not** and **may not**.

✈ **May not** is never contracted. (We don't say **mayn't**.)

✈ **Might not** is usually not contracted. (**Mightn't** is rarely used.)

✈ **Could not** is a Modal of Probability: See Unit 11.

✈ **Couldn't** is a Modal of Past Prohibition. See Unit 2.

10.11 *April may not stay overnight in Bombay. She wants to hurry up and get to Gujarat.*

10.12 *The caves at Ajanta and Ellora might not stay open after dark. We should go during the day.*

10.13 *We may not have paid too much for that scarf. Another shopkeeper had one for the same price.*

10.14 *Angela and Nisha might not have gone to the camel market in Pushkar. If they didn't go, maybe they'll go with us tomorrow.*

Spoken English: Might Have and Could Have

Might have is pronounced **mighta** in informal spoken English.
Could have is pronounced **coulda**.

10.15 *Dave mighta spent the night in Udaipur.*

10.16 *Sandra and Vijya coulda taken the bus to Kodaikanal.*

Exercises

Exercise A. Rewrite the sentences using may, might or could.

1. It's possible that it will rain tomorrow. That would really spoil our plans!
    It may (might or could) rain tomorrow. That would really spoil our plans.

2. Maybe she'll go swimming later today.

3. Perhaps he's finished with the exam by now. He's been doing it for two hours.

4. Maybe Radeesh won't have enough money to visit Calcutta.

5. It's possible that Manoj will want to eat *vadai* for breakfast.

6. Maybe she'll call next week.

7. Perhaps Diane doesn't know when Ismail will return from his trip to Jaipur.

8. Maybe they won't stay in the Maharajah's palace in Udaipur because it's expensive.

9. It's possible that Raju and Mona are too tired to walk to the Red Fort.

10. Perhaps Francis and Antonio aren't going to Agra tomorrow.

Exercise B. Rewrite the above sentences in the past tense. Remember to change all expressions of time from the present and future to the past.

1. _____

2. _____

3. _____

4. _____

5. _____

6. _____

7. _____

8. _____

9. _____

10. _____

Exercise C. Read the situations. Then write three sentences explaining the possibilities of what happened.

1. A woman is pale. She is holding her stomach.

   She might have eaten bad food last night.

   She could have gotten a cramp from exercising.

   She may have drunk some contaminated water.

2. A man in an expensive suit is lying on the sidewalk.

   _____

   _____

   _____

3. There is blood on the floor in front of an apartment door.

_____

_____

_____

4. A small girl is standing in a park crying.

_____

_____

_____

5. You receive a letter, but there is nothing inside the envelope.

_____

_____

_____

6. People are running out of a bank and screaming.

_____

_____

_____

7. Many students are sleeping in class.

_____

_____

_____

8. Two people are dancing in the street.

_____

_____

_____

Exercise D. Read the situations. Write three possibilities about what might happen next.

1. Ed always comes to work late.

   He might lose his job.

   The manager may buy him an alarm clock.

   He could receive a warning from his boss.

2. You forgot to turn off your oven before you left the house.

   _____

   _____

   _____

3. You leave your briefcase in a taxicab.

   _____

   _____

   _____

4. The airline loses your luggage.

   _____

   _____

   _____

5. The train stops running before you get to your destination.

   _____

   _____

   _____

6. Your car runs out of gas on a lonely road.

_____

_____

_____

7. Ten people come to your house for dinner, but you only invited five.

_____

_____

_____

8. You're on the 10th floor of a building and there's a fire.

_____

_____

_____

9. You open your door and there's a baby in a basket outside.

_____

_____

_____

Exercise E. Imagine that you are going to these places. Who might you see there? What might you do? Write three sentences telling them what's possible in each of the cities and countries.

1. Mumbai (Bombay)

   You might hear many different languages.

   You might see many Indian movie actors and actresses.

   You might eat spicy food.

2. Disney World

   _____

   _____

   _____

3. London

   _____

   _____

   _____

4. New York City

   _____

   _____

   _____

5. Paris

   _____

   _____

   _____

6. Tokyo

_____

_____

_____

7. Rome

_____

_____

_____

8. The moon

_____

_____

_____

Exercise F. Unscramble the sentences.

1. morning/may/this/rained/it/have

   It may have rained this morning.

2. sun looks gotten Ajay sick he may because much have too

3. far because is driveway might too home car the Sridevi gone from her in have not

4. may the when went red the been blue the through light accident caused car have

5. when visit Ravi watch to comes could game he to baseball to a want

Exercise G. Read the story. After you read, underline all the Modals of Possibility.

It Might Rain

Anita opened the curtains and looked out into the sunny yard. "Ashok," she said, "it's a beautiful day today. Let's go to the beach."

Ashok, who was just waking up and who had been looking forward to a relaxing day at home, replied, "I listened to the weather report on the news last night, and they said it might rain."

"Oh, come on, Ashok, you can't always believe those weather reports. Look out the window. The sun is up and the birds are out. It's lovely." She put on her robe and went downstairs.

An hour later, Ashok was still sleeping. Anita was thinking how she might get him out of bed without going upstairs to wake him. She decided to vacuum the living room with their noisy old vacuum cleaner. She plugged it in and turned it on. The noise sounded like the noise of a jackhammer at a construction site. She whistled to herself while she vacuumed. Ashok may have heard the noise, but he didn't came downstairs.

Another hour passed, and Anita was wondering how her husband could stay in bed on such a wonderful morning.

"He may not have heard the vacuum," she thought to herself, "but this could be the thing to get him out of bed." She put her favorite CD in the stereo, knowing that Ashok hated it. "This will get him downstairs. The vacuum might not have bothered him, but he hates this music, and he'll definitely want to turn it off." She turned up the volume and continued cleaning the house.

Another hour passed, and still there was no sign of Ashok. Anita decided that she would go upstairs herself and wake him up. This was ridiculous — wasting a beautiful day like this so he could sleep.

When she entered the room, she was shocked. The bed was made, the window was open, and Ashok was not in either the bedroom or the bathroom. He was gone.

She went to the window and looked out into the yard. The sky was getting darker, and a raindrop hit her hand.

Questions. Answer with modals of possibility.

1. Where did Ashok go?

2. How did he leave without Anita seeing him?

Write your own ending to the story…

(Answers on page 127)

A Trip to Mexico

Should, Ought to
→ Use these to express an expectation. Based on evidence, something is very certain of occurring. It may not occur, but it probably will.
→ Use **should not** for a negative expectation. **Ought not to** is used infrequently.

11.1 *María should be home by now. Her flight to Monterrey was supposed to land at 4 o'clock.*

11.2 *Pablo ought to be back from the party. It's already 2:00 a.m., and he has school tomorrow.*

Must, Have to, Have got to
→ Use these to express an inference. This is a conclusion based on specific evidence or information. It is more certain than an expectation.

11.3 *Sunsets must be colorful on the Baja Peninsula. Look at these beautiful postcards.*

11.4 *Oaxaca has to have the best-made rugs in Mexico. All the tourists buy them.*

11.5 *Christmas has got to be the busiest time of year in Acapulco and Puerto Vallarta.*

Can't, Couldn't

✈ Use these to express negative probability. This is something that is certain of **not happening**.

11.6 *That person can't be Juan. He lives in Argentina now.*

11.7 *You couldn't possibly eat more tortillas and beans for breakfast. You've eaten three plates already.*

Past: Should, Ought to, Must, Have to, Can't, Couldn't

✈ Make the past form by adding **have + past participle**.

11.8 *It should have been a quick trip from Nogales to Las Mochis, but we ran out of gas near Hermosillo.*

11.9 *You must have traveled on the bus all night. You look awful!*

11.10 *Leslie had to have changed more money. She's buying more jewelry in the market.*

11.11 *Gabriela couldn't have been sick because she was at the party with Ricardo last night.*

Negative Forms: Be careful!

✈ Don't confuse negative probability with Modals of Prohibition.
See Unit 3: Modals of Prohibition.

✈ **Have to** has no negative form. **Don't/doesn't have to** is used for no obligation.
See Chapter 4: Modals of Obligation.

11.12 *Estéban must not like rice and beans. He hasn't touched them.*   Probability

11.13 *Estéban mustn't eat beans and rice. They're bad for his stomach.*   Prohibition

11.14 *Estéban doesn't have to eat his beans and rice.*   No Obligation

Spoken English: Should have, Ought to, Must Have, Have got to

✈ **Should have** is pronounced **shoulda** in informal spoken English.

✈ **Ought to** is pronounced **oughta** in informal spoken English.

✈ **Have to** and **has to** are pronounced **hafta** and **hasta** in informal spoken English.

✈ **Must have** is pronounced **musta** in informal spoken English.

✈ **Have got to** is pronounced **gotta** in informal spoken English.

✈ **Couldn't have** is pronounced **couldna** in informal spoken English.

Exercise A. Use **should** or **ought to** to complete the sentences.

1. Jean _____ be in her office by now, but I'm never really sure what time she comes in.

2. They _____ to be in Cancún by now, if the plane arrived on time.

3. The door is open, so the doctor _____ be ready to see another patient.

4. The beans _____ be done, but taste them first to make sure.

5. They _____ enjoy the Parque Chapultepec because there are some interesting things to see and do there.

Exercise B. Use **must, have to, can't** or **couldn't** to complete the sentences.

1. José _____ be bullfighting in the Plaza de Toros because he broke his leg last week.

2. Elena _____ be here because her gloves and coat are on the chair over there.

3. Spanish class _____ be over already! It seems like it just started.

4. Elise and Andy are going to Mazatlán for the winter? You _____ be kidding. You know they have to stay in Vermont.

5. They _____ not have eaten because all of the food is still on the stove.

Exercise C. Use **should/ought to** (Expectation) or **must/have to** (Inference) to complete the sentences.

1. Paula ___must (has to)___ be in her office now. I can hear her talking in there.

   Paula ___should (ought to)___ be in her office now, but I'm not really sure.

2. Angela and Jorge _____ have landed in Mexico City already because they just called.

   Angela and Jorge _____ have landed in Mexico City already, but the weather has been bad and many flights have been delayed.

3. The soup _____ be done by now. Why don't you taste it and make sure?

   The soup _____ be done by now. The recipe says it should cook for an hour.

4. They _____ be here because they told me they were coming.

   They _____ be here because I saw their car in the parking lot.

5. There's the phone! It _____ be your mother. She said she'd call sometime today.

   There's the phone! It _____ be your mother. She always calls at 7:30 on Tuesday.

6. That _____ be my son practicing piano. It sounds like him.

   That _____ be my son practicing piano. He always plays that part wrong.

7. The Bulls _____ have won that game because they were ahead for most of the game.

   The Bulls _____ have won that game because their fans were celebrating outside the stadium.

Exercise D. Change the sentences from the present to the past. Don't forget to make all of the necessary changes.

1. They should be ready by 8:00 because the train for Chihuahua leaves at 8:15.
   They should have been ready at 8:00 because the train for Chihuahua left at 8:15.

2. Patricio can't be in Hermosillo. He doesn't have a reservation until next Wednesday.

3. Alejandra and Maria ought to be at the party tonight because they love to dance.

4. He must not like me very much. He never calls.

5. My brother couldn't be in Monterrey. He lives 1,000 miles from here.

6. You can't be serious when you say that you're leaving me forever.

Exercise E. Put the words in the "scrambled" sentences in the correct order. The first word in the sentence may not be capitalized.

1. Thailand be from has a friend this to my letter.

2. doctor the be office his now ought in to.

3. summer have time next should I visit to you.

4. not studied exam the students the must for have.

5. my been sister Japan conference have couldn't in at the.

Exercise F. Read the newspaper headlines. Write three reasons to explain how each event happened. Use **must, have to, must not, can't** or **couldn't**.

1. Giraffe Found in Swimming Pool

   Someone must have left the cage door at the zoo open.

   The giraffe had to have been very hot.

   The giraffe couldn't have used a key to escape from the zoo.

2. Building Falls Down

   _____

   _____

   _____

3. Car Explodes

   _____

   _____

   _____

4. Teacher Collapses in Class

   _____

   _____

   _____

5. Mouse & Cat Help Police Catch Thieves

   _____

   _____

   _____

Exercise G. Complete the sentences with the appropriate Modal of Probability.
  Some sentences may have more than one correct answer. Be prepared to explain why.

1. The car keys _have to (must)_ be in my purse. I always put them there.

2. If you go to the desert in June, you _____ need too many clothes.

3. That _____ be a local fruit because the climate's not warm enough
    to grow them here.

4. They _____ gone on vacation because their newspapers are piled up
    on the porch.

5. We _____ be there by nine because it only takes two hours to get
    there, and we plan on leaving at seven.

6. Her office is still open, so she _____ gone home yet.

7. He _____ read the book already. I only gave it to him last night.

8. She _____ been married then because she went out with her friends
    every night.

9. He looks really young, but he _____ be old enough. Otherwise he
    wouldn't be working here.

10. Brad _____ be almost finished with his book by now. He's been
    working on it for nearly twenty years.

Exercise H. Read the story about a report of a missing person. Underline all the Modals of Probability.

The Missing Person

This story took place in Detective Dave Estano's office at the Ridge Road Police Department. It was 8 a.m. on a Monday morning. It was a very hot day when someone knocked on Detective Estano's door.

"Come in," said Estano.

"Hello, my name is Addison Miller. I'd like to report a missing person."

"Please sit down, Ms. Miller and tell me all about it."

"Well, you see, I went to my sister Lauren's house last night at 10 p.m. She told me to come over. I hadn't seen her for about a week or two."

"Do you talk to her often?"

"Oh, yes, we talk on the phone every day."

"OK. So tell me about last night."

"Well, as I said, I went to her house at ten o'clock, and no one was there. She couldn't have gone out without calling me or leaving me a note. She's not like that. She never goes out alone at night. Something must have happened to her."

"Well, Ms. Miller, maybe something came up suddenly, and she had to leave."

"No, she couldn't have had something else to do. Something serious had to have happened to her. I'm very worried. She didn't come home at all last night. She should be home by now. She ought to be there, but she isn't."

"I'm sure there's a logical explanation for this. If she's not home yet, I'm sure she'll be home any time now."

"I told you she ought to be there, but she isn't. Something terrible had to have happened to her. I know it. I feel like something's very wrong."

"Listen, Ms. Miller. If it makes you feel any better, I'll go over to her house with you. We can see if anything looks out of place."

"Thanks a lot, Detective. I must be overtired or something to be reacting like this. And the heat is really getting to me. I just have this feeling that something bad must have happened."

They drove to Lauren's house. The house was in a nice part of the city with a lot of trees and beautiful homes overlooking the bay. They used Addison's key to open the door.

"What's this?" Detective Estano asked as he stepped into the house. He leaned over and picked up a piece of paper off the floor. "It's got your name on it. It looks like it's a note for you."

"It's from Lauren," sighed Addison as she took the note from Detective Estano. "This explains everything. Thanks so much for taking the time to help me out. You can't imagine how relieved I am."

"It's always a pleasure to help out, Ms. Miller. I'll give you a ride back to the station so you can pick up your car."

Questions

1. What do you think happened to Arlene?
2. What was written in the note that Detective Estano found?

Write the conversation between Lauren and Addison when they see each other again.

(Answers on page 127)

A Trip to Germany

Used to & Would

➔   Use these to express habitual actions in the past. A habitual action is
something that was done many times or that was part of someone's life.

12.1 *On our way to school every morning, we **used to walk** past the Brandenburg Gate.
Ingrid and I **would walk** that way every morning. We loved growing up in Berlin.*

Used to & Would

➔   Use **used to** for a repeated action or a condition that was true in the past,
but that is no longer true. It is often used with verbs such as *have, want, live,
love,* and *like.*

➔   **Used to** is also usually used wth sense verbs: *seem, feel, look, taste, smell.*

➔   Use **would** only for a repeated action in the past.

12.2 *Isolde used to live in Regensburg, but now she lives in Dresden.*
    (Past true condition)
12.3 *When we lived in Hamburg, we used to watch the ships.*
    (Repeated action)
12.4 *As a student In Leipzig, I would often read in the library until midnight.*
    (Repeated Action)

Note the uses of **used to** and **would** in the following story:

*I remember a high school trip to Germany. We went during our spring vacation. We stayed in Munich, and the spring weather was beautiful. Ralph and I **used to get** up early every morning and walk around the quiet streets. After we walked for about an hour, we **would stop** in a café and have cake and coffee. Ralph **would always eat** two pieces of cake. He said walking made him hungry. Of course, eating the cake made him gain weight.*

*When we got back to school from our trip, Ralph tried to play on the baseball team, but Mr. Evans, the coach, told him he was too big. Ralph joined the school newspaper instead. He **used to write** beautiful articles. Now, he's a famous writer. He still visits Germany every year and eats two pieces of cake for breakfast.*

Questions
➔ Make questions with **use to** and **did**. **Would** is used less frequently in questions.

12.5 *Did Franz use to study in Dresden?*
       No, he didn't. He used to study in Frankfurt.

12.6 *Where did Monika use to work?*
       She used to work at a company in Bonn.

12.7 *When you lived there, where would you go and what would you do on weekends?*

Negatives
➔ Note the position of **not** in the examples.
➔ Contract **would not** to **wouldn't** and **did not use to** to **didn't use to**.

12.8 *When we lived in Berlin, we didn't use to stay out late.*

12.9 *Jurgen and Ilka wouldn't drive when they were in Germany. They thought people drove too fast on the Autobahn. They would take the train.*

Be Careful! Used to & Be used to
➔ Don't confuse **used to** and **be used to**. They are not the same. You have seen that **used to** refers to habitual actions in the past.
➔ Use **be used to** to talk about being accustomed to something.
➔ **Be used to** uses a form of "be" and a verb + ing after it. It can also be used in the present or future, and it may occur with "get" in place of "be," for example, "You'll get used to the climate."

12.10 *I used to travel to Germany every year, but now I don't.*
        (This is a past habitual action.)
12.11 *When I first arrived in Germany, I wasn't used to traveling by train.*
        (This is something the speaker was or was not **accustomed to doing** in the past.)

Exercises

Exercise A. Match the appropriate parts of the sentences in the left and right columns.

Beginning of Sentence	*End of Sentence*
1. They used to live in Frankfurt, ( )	a. I used to drink beer when I lived in Munich.
2. When Emma lived in Heidelberg, ( )	b. deer used to live on that land.
3. When I lived on the farm outside Munich, ( )	c. but now in Magdeburg she stays home every night.
4. Barbara used to like to walk around Karlsruhe late at night, ( )	d. they used to ride their bicycles to work.
5. Although I preferred to drink coffee at the university, ( )	e. but they live in Arizona now because it's warmer.
6. Marjorie used to have long hair, ( )	f. we would wake up at 4:30 in the morning and begin working.
7. Stan and Ginger would travel every summer ( )	g. I would stay awake all night.
8. Before the new shopping center was built, ( )	h. but she keeps it short now.
9. Because Inge and Wolfgang didn't have a car, ( )	i. she would visit the castle as often as possible.
10. When I studied for my exams at the university, ( )	j. when they were younger.

Exercise B. Fill in the blanks with *used to or would.* Some of the sentences have more than one correct answer.

1. Travis _____ used to _____ work as a lawyer, but now he has his own business.

2. The twins _____ get up early and milk the cows before breakfast.

3. Every day at 4:00, I _____ go to a small café and relax with a cup of coffee. I _____ read the newspaper and write letters.

4. Heinz _____ have a horse, and he _____ ride every day.

5. When Heidi visited her parents, she _____ sleep in the small room upstairs.

6. During the summer, I _____ take long walks in the Black Forest.

7. The brass band _____ play every Saturday night in the town square. My mother _____ take me to the concert.

Exercise C. Write one Wh- question, one Yes-No question and one Negative sentence for the sentences given.

1. Katie used to live near the church in Dresden.

   Where did Katie use to live? _____ (Question)

   Did Katie use to live in Dresden? _____ (Yes/No Question)

   Katie didn't use to live in Dresden. _____ (Negative Sentence)

2. The Hoeferts used to eat a big meal every evening.

   When _____ (Question)

   _____ (Yes/No Question)

   _____ (Negative Sentence)

3. Franz used to wear glasses.

   What _____ (Question)

   _____ (Yes/No Question)

   _____ (Negative Sentence)

4. My mother, my sister and I would get up at 6:00 and walk in the park.

   When _____ (Question)

   _____ (Yes/No Question)

   _____ (Negative Sentence)

5. Reggie used to go skiing in the Alps every winter.

   Where _____ (Question)

   _____ (Yes/No Question)

   _____ (Negative Sentence)

6. Christine and I would hike every Tuesday afternoon.

What _____ (Question)

_____ (Yes/No Question)

_____ (Negative Sentence)

7. Students used to do their presentations on the last day of the course.

When _____ (Question)

_____ (Yes/No Question)

_____ (Negative Sentence)

8. Art and Joan used to be good friends before they got married and divorced.

Who _____ (Question)

_____ (Yes/No Question)

_____ (Negative Sentence)

Exercise D. Complete the sentences with your own information. Write at least three sentences about things you used to or would do.

1. When I was a child,

   _____

   _____

   _____

   _____

2. When I was a student,

   _____

   _____

   _____

   _____

3. During school vacations,

   _____

   _____

   _____

   _____

4. Before I began studying English,

   _____

   _____

   _____

   _____

Exercise E. Imagine that you are 100 and that the year is 2065. What did and didn't you used to do? Write three sentences for every decade of your life.

0-10 years old

_____

_____

_____

_____

10-20 years old

_____

_____

_____

_____

20-30 years old

_____

_____

_____

_____

30-40 years old

_____

_____

_____

_____

40-50 years old

_____

_____

_____

_____

50-60 years old

_____

_____

_____

_____

60-70 years old

_____

_____

_____

_____

70-80 years old

_____

_____

_____

_____

Exercise F. Read the story *From My Grandfather*. After you read, underline all the Modals of Habitual Action.

From My Grandfather: Remembering the Old Days

Looking back over the past 90 years of my life, I often think about how things used to be. I know it's foolish to be nostalgic, but I really do enjoy remembering all the things I used to do when I was a young man.

I would always get up before the sun because there was always so much to do. We lived on a farm, and I would milk the cows, clean the barn and feed the chickens before breakfast. I used to love the way the sunlight sparkled on the fields. Now, there are houses and condominiums where all those fields used to be.

When I was out there alone in the morning, I used to stand quietly and listen to the birds chirping in the trees and the roosters crowing in the distance. I would listen for the roosters and my neighbors on the other farms. We all would get up at about the same time and do pretty much the same things. When I heard the church bells strike 6:00, I would go inside the house, wash up and have a big breakfast.

My mother was a wonderful cook. In the summer, on my way into the house, I could smell the breakfast before I got there. She used to make me pancakes and eggs and fresh coffee, but she wouldn't eat with me. She would only watch me and my father and brothers and make sure we had everything we needed.

After lunch I would work outdoors until lunchtime. I used to be so happy when Ma finally called us in to eat. I would work so hard that I had the appetite of two men.

But, you know, even though I have wonderful memories of living on that farm, our lives there were difficult. We would work long and hard hours, and we lived a very simple life. My cousins from the city used to visit, and I remember thinking that I might like to live there one day.

I would dream about leaving the farm, but I never did. I used to think about what life would be like if I could get away. I used to wonder about all the things I might do. Now, the future has come and gone. It's part of my past now. And, just think, that boy in the field listening to the roosters and birds used to imagine that the future would never arrive soon enough.

(Answers on page 129)

A Trip to Turkey

What are Direct & Indirect Speech?

- Direct Speech is what one person says to another in speech or writing.
- Indirect (Reported) Speech is what another person "reports" (tells a third person) about the direct conversation. It is used with verbs such as *say* and *tell*. *Ask* is used in questions.

What happens to Modal Verbs in Indirect Speech?

- Indirect Speech is a "report of what someone said" and should be in the past in formal written English.
- Note the changes in the modal verbs below when they are used in indirect speech. The other modals do not change.

Modals of Ability	can ⇒	**could**
Modals of Prohibition	mustn't ⇒	**couldn't**
Modals of Obligation	has to ⇒	**had to**
	am/are/is to⇒	**was/were to**
Modals of the Future	will ⇒	**would**
	am/are/is going to ⇒	**was going to** or **were going to**
Modals of Possibility	may ⇒	**might**
Modals of Probability	have to ⇒	**had to**

13.1 *"When will you go to Istanbul?" Cathleen asked.*   Direct Speech (with *ask*)
Cathleen asked when I would go to Istanbul.   Indirect Speech (Future)

13.2 *"Scott may visit us in Ankara," Ahmet said.*   Direct Speech (with *say*)
Ahmet said Scott might visit us in Ankara.   Indirect Speech (Possibility)

13.3 *"Helmut is going to see Dolmabahçe," Hans said.*   Direct Speech (with *say*)
Hans said Helmut was going to see Dolmabahçe.   Indirect Speech (Future)

13.4 *"I can't wait to go to Ephesus," Carol told me.*   Direct Speech (with *tell*)
Carol told me she couldn't wait to go to Ephesus.   Indirect Speech (Ability)

13.5 *"You have to see Pamukkale," Nur told me.*   Direct speech (with *tell*)
Nur told me I had to see Pamukkale.   Indirect Speech (Obligation)

Note
→   When a Modal Verb is already in the past, do not change its form.
See the examples below.

13.6 *"I could have danced all night at that club on the*
Bosphorus," Sasha said.   Direct
Sasha said he could have danced all night.   Indirect (Possibility)

13.7 *"Lake Van must have been cold in the winter,"*   Direct
Igor remarked to Olga.
Igor remarked to Olga that Lake Van must have been
cold in the winter.   Indirect (Probability)

13.8 *"You should have visited the Hagia Sofia," Gülen said.*   Direct
Gülen said I should have visited the Hagia Sofia.   Indirect (Advisability)

Be Careful! Spoken & Written English
→   Spoken English is more informal than written English.
→   Modal Verbs don't **always** change to their past forms in spoken English.
See the examples below.

13.9 *"I can meet you at Topkapi tomorrow," Beti said.*
Beti said she can meet us at Topkapi tomorrow.   Spoken
Beti said she could meet us at Topkapi tomorrow.   Written

13.10 *"Will you watch the sunset on the Aegean?" Kumiko asked me.*
Kumiko asked me if I will watch the sunset on the Aegean.   Spoken
Kumiko asked me if I would watch the sunset on the Aegean.   Written
(Yes-No questions use "if" in Indirect Speech.)

Exercises

Exercise A. Change the Direct Speech statements to Indirect Speech.
Remember to make all necessary time and pronoun changes.

1. "I can't believe how beautiful Bolu is in the autumn," Jeannie said.

   _____

2. "We shouldn't wait too long to buy our World Cup tickets," Hisham said to Ahmed.

   _____

3. "You mustn't call home too many times because you'll get homesick," Burak said.

   _____

4. "You must remember not to miss our trip to the Blue Mosque," Nancy said.

   _____

5. "I 'll have a cup of Turkish coffee," Mrs. Hamilton told the waiter.

   _____

6. "Carrie and Alexandra are going to go to Erzurum on Monday," Nihal said.

   _____

7. "I'll see you in September," Bill told Nuri.

   _____

8. "Ayla has to call me this weekend," Hülya told me.

   _____

9. "Edgar may stop in Edirne, on his way to Greece," Phil said.

   _____

10. "You have to be crazy if you think I want to spend the holiday with your
    family!" he said to his wife. *(Be careful of this one. There are a lot of changes.)*

   _____

Exercise B. Change the Direct Speech statements to Indirect Speech. Remember to make all necessary time and pronoun changes.

1. "What time will you leave tomorrow?" Jeannie asked Aydin.

    _____

2. "Why do I have to go to Gallipoli alone?" Hisham asked Ahmed.

    _____

3. "Should I visit the Tetrapylon when I'm in Aphrodisias?" John asked me.

    _____

4. "Would you like to go to a taverna?" Sevim asked Nancy.

    _____

5. "Are you going to go to Capadocia?" Jeremy asked Toru.

    _____

6. "Where will you stay in Bursa?" Bruce asked.

    _____

7. "Can you speak Turkish well?" Bill asked Heidi.

    _____

8. "Where should I eat when I visit Izmir?" Paulina asked Deniz.

    _____

9: "Do you want to go to Bodrum with me?" Ray asked us.

    _____

10. "Do we have to carry our passports in Turkey?" Khamees and Abdulla asked.

    _____

(Answers on page 130)

A Trip to Italy

What are Conditionals?

A conditional sentence is an "If" clause and a result clause.
There are two types of conditional sentences: Real and Unreal.
Unreal Conditionals are also called Hypothetical Conditionals.
Real Conditionals use the present-future time.
Unreal Conditionals have two time frames: the present-future and the past.
Modal Verbs are used to change the meanings of the result clauses.

Real Conditionals

Look at the following examples. The meaning of the result clauses changes
depending on the modal verb.

14.1 *If Angelo visits Italy, . . .*

. . .he can go to the Colosseum and the Spanish Steps.	(Ability)
. . .he should see St. Peter's Basilica and the Vatican museum.	(Advisability)
. . .he mustn't rent a car because he's not a very good driver.	(Prohibition)
. . .he must visit the Amalfi Coast because it's beautiful.	(Obligation)
. . .he will stay with his brother near the Quirinale.	(Future)
. . .he may learn to like a two-hour lunch.	(Possibility)
. . .he must have more time and money than I think he has.	(Probability)Unreal

---

> ### *Conditionals in the Present-Future:* **would, could or might**
> Unreal conditional sentences are not true at the time of speaking. They might be true in the future, but first the "If..." condition must happen.
>
> Use **would** for willingness/intent, **could** for ability and **might** for possibility.
>
> Other modal meanings are generally not used.

14.2 *If Elena visited Italy, she would spend all of her time in museums.*
14.3 *If Francesca and Balndina came to Rome to study, they could live with their aunt.*
14.4 *If Jason wanted breakfast early, he might walk down to the cappuccino bar next to his hotel.*

> ### *Unreal Conditionals in the Past:* **would have, could have or might have**
> Like the Present-Future Unreal Conditionals, these sentences were not true in the past. They could have been true, but the "If..." condition did not happen.
>
> Use **would have** for willingness/intent, **could have** for ability and **might have** for possibility.
>
> Other modal meanings are generally not used.

14.5 *If Paul had gone to Italy in the spring, he would have seen many wildflowers.*
14.6 *If Alia and Troy had brought more money, they could have stayed in a nicer hotel in Palermo.*
14.7 *If we hadn't taken the train to Calabria, we wouldn't have seen very much of the country.*

Exercise A. Complete the Real Conditional sentences with a result clause.

Exercises

Use the modal meaning in parentheses.

1. If Ahmed doesn't like spaghetti, _____ . (Ability)

2. If you visit Sicily, _____ . (Advisability)

3. If Eleanor wants to work in Milan, _____ . (Obligation)

4. If I need money in Rome, _____ . (Future)

5. If I rent a car, _____ . (Probability)

6. If Jean and Leslie don't go to Rome, _____ . (Possibility)

7. If Sergio doesn't visit the Trevi Fountain, _____ .(Advisability)

8. If we visit Pompei, _____ . (Obligation)

9. If Amanda and Gina buy train passes, _____ . (Ability)

10. If you want a romantic evening in Venice, _____ . (Prohibition)

Exercise B. Complete the Unreal Conditional sentences with a result clause.
Use the modal meaning in parentheses. Be careful of the time in each sentence.

1. If I visited my family during the holidays, _____

_____ . (Willingness)

2. If Paolo studied art in Florence, _____

_____ . (Ability)

3. If Lucia traveled alone to Sorrento, _____

_____ . (Possibility)

4. If Mark and Roger had missed their flight, _____

_____ . (Possibility)

5. If Lydia and Loretta had learned Italian well, _____

_____ . (Ability)

6. If I lost my passport, _____

_____ . (Willingness)

7. If Patricio and Louisa hadn't gone on a tour of Herculaneum, _____

_____ . (Possibility)

8. If Diane wanted to eat good spaghetti, _____

_____ . (Ability)

9. If I knew more about art, _____

_____ . (Willingness)

10. If I had known that you'd be so late, _____

_____ . (Ability)

Exercise C. Write your own sentences using the given 1) type of conditional, 2) time, and 3) the modal meaning.

1. Real/Present-future/Advisability

2. Unreal/Past/Willingness

3. Unreal/Present-future/Possibility

4. Unreal/Present-future/Ability

5. Real/Present-future/Future

6. Real/Present-future/Obligation

7. Real/Present-future/Prohibition

8. Unreal/Past/Possibility

9. Unreal/Present-future/Ability

10. Real/Present-future/Probability

(Answers on page 131)

APPENDIX

Answer Key

Unit 1: ABILITY/EGYPT

Exercise A *page 2*

I can't.
I don't know how to swim.
I can't ride a bike, either.
I can't see without my glasses.
We can play some music.
I know how to play guitar, and you can sing with me.
Maybe you'll be able to play, but I certainly won't be able to sing.
I really can't sing at all.

Exercise B *(Possible Answers)* *page 3*

1. A musician can read music. *(A musician is able to read music.)*
   A musician can play many instruments.
   A musician can sing very well.

2. A doctor can see many patients.
   A doctor can understand many diseases.
   A doctor can give good advice to her patients.

3. A mother can take care of her children.
   A mother can work very hard outside the house.
   A mother can prepare the dinner.

4. A tour guide can show tourists many ancient temples.
   A tour guide can help tourists buy souvenirs.
   A tour guide can explain the history of a city to tourists.

5. A police officer can help people.
   A police officer can write parking tickets.
   A police officer can investigate crimes.

6. A taxi driver in Cairo can take tourists to the Pyramids.
   A taxi driver in Cairo can drive in a lot of traffic.
   A taxi driver in Cairo can show you many interesting sites in Egypt.

Exercise C *(Possible Answers)* *page 4*

I can speak English. (I am able to...)
I can play the piano.
I can ride a bicycle.
I can run three miles.
I can visit my friends.

I can't ride a horse. (I'm not able to...)
I can't speak Italian.
I can't see without my glasses.
I can't cook very well.
I can't write in Arabic.

Exercise D *page 4*

1. Daughter: couldn't/wasn't able to...

2. Boss: Could you/Were you able to...?

3. Co-worker 1: couldn't/wasn't able to...
   Co-worker 2: could...

4. Friend 2: couldn't/wasn't able to...
   couldn't/wasn't able to...

5. Father: couldn't
   couldn't

6. Sister 2: couldn't/wasn't able to...

Exercise E *page 5*

2. Was your friend able to run fast (before)?
   Yes, she/he was.
   No, she/he wasn't.
3. Could Metwally and Omar play the piano (last year)?
   Yes, they could.
   No, they couldn't.
4. Did Khalid know how to do many things on the computer (last September)?
   Yes, he did.
   No, he didn't.
5. Was Rafik able to travel to many countries (when he was young)?
   Yes, he was.
   No, he wasn't.

Exercise G *page 6*

1. Next year, I will be able to speak Arabic very well.
2. CORRECT
   3. Alia will be able to play the piano...
4. CORRECT
5. I will be able to belly dance...
6. CORRECT
7. CORRECT
8. You will be able to drive...
9. CORRECT
10. Ali will be able to paint...

Exercise H *(Possible Answers)* *page 7*

1. I couldn't drive a car. (I wasn't able to drive...)
2. I could talk on the telephone.
3. I could work on my farm.
4. I couldn't watch TV.
5. I could relax with my family and neighbors.

1. I'll be able to see my friend when we talk on the telephone.
2. I'll be able to spend the weekend on the moon.

3. I'll be able to eat food from a tube.
4. I'll be able to stay in my house and do everything.
5. I'll be able to drive a space ship.

Exercise I *page 8*

I can see his dark wooden house...
...he can do magical things.
They say he can make things appear and disappear at any time.
He can become invisible and walk through the village streets...
...and no one is able to see him.
He knows how to grow beautiful flowers outside...
...he can talk to wild animals.
...he can understand what the animals say to him.
...he can do.
I often wonder how he is able to stay alive...
How can he live that way?
How is he able to survive the long years and hard winters alone?
How can I answer them?
I can't.
I can only continue looking for him...
...one day I'll be able to meet him and ask these questions myself.

UNIT 2: PROHIBITION/ECUADOR

Exercise A *page 10*

2. You mustn't/can't wear... (People mustn't/can't...)
3. You mustn't/can't take...
4. You mustn't/can't park...
5. You mustn't/can't throw...
6. You mustn't/can't eat...
7. You mustn't/can't wear...
8. You mustn't/can't cut

Exercise B *(Possible Answers)* *page 10*

1. You can't/mustn't have too much luggage.
   You can't/mustn't pack a gun in your suitcase.
   You can't/mustn't smoke in the departure lounge.

2. You can't/mustn't smoke cigarettes.
   You can't/mustn't talk loud in the waiting room.
   You can't/mustn't arrive after the visiting hours.

3. You can't/mustn't call on the weekends.
   You can't/mustn't enter without a passport.
   You can't/mustn't take photographs inside.

4. You can't/mustn't take something without paying for it.
   You can't/mustn't eat food while you shop.
   You can't/mustn't open the packages.

5. You can't/mustn't forget to bring your notebook.
   You can't/mustn't talk when other students are speaking.
   You can't/mustn't sleep.

Exercise C *(Possible Answers)* *page 11*

2. You mustn't smoke because my mother doesn't allow it.
3. You're not permitted to take photos here because it's forbidden
4. You can't park here because this is reserved for the president.
5. You are not allowed to climb that fence because it is dangerous.
6. You cannot talk in here because it's a study area.

Exercise E *page 13*

2. You mustn't wear your shoes in temples in Thailand.
3. We cannot use a flash in this museum.
4. The students were forbidden to use their notes during the exam.
5. When I was young, I was not permitted to ride my bicycle in the street.
6. You mustn't go out after dark because there is a curfew.
7. In the U.S., you are not allowed to drink in a bar if you are under 21 years old.

Exercise F *page 14*

You can't take photos in here. = mustn't
I'm sorry, ma'am, but it's not allowed. = not permitted
Photography is not permitted in this museum. = not allowed
I know we mustn't touch the exhibits, and we mustn't lean on the glass cases... =can't

UNIT 3: ADVISABILITY/

THAILAND

Exercise A *page 18*

2. should/ought to/had better
3. should/ought to/had better
   should not (shouldn't)
4. Should...?
5. should
6. should/ought to
7. should
8. should not (shouldn't)
   should/ought to
   should/ought to

Exercise B *page 18*

1. a	4. f	7. i	9. e
2. d	5. h	8. c	10. j
3. g	6. b		

Exercise C *(Possible Answers)* *page 19*

2. She should have practiced more outside class.
3. He should have gotten up earlier.
4. She should have done her homework.
5. They shouldn't have drunk coffee.
6. He shouldn't have had plastic surgery.
7. She should have asked a question.
8. She shouldn't have driven so fast.
9. We should have gone shopping.
10. I should have made my reservation earlier.

Exercise F *page 23*

What should I do now?
Hey, Mister, you ought to slow down.
You should go back to driving school.
You should use an umbrella on a night like this.
Why don't you watch where you're going?
You really should be more careful.
You should have something to drink and relax a little.
What I really should do is take a long vacation.
You should get a raise for this.
And you should go into the men's room and dry off.
While you're there, you ought to comb your hair, too.
I ought to listen to you more often.
Yeah, you should.
You should worry about keeping the job you have.
And you had better hurry up, too, because the real boss just walked in the front door.
He'd better get a whole new life!

UNIT 4: OBLIGATION AND NECESSITY/JAPAN

Exercise A *page 27*

2. You have to/must stop at all red lights.
3. You have to/must speak only English in class.
4. You have to/must chew your food well before swallowing it.
5. You have to/must watch your luggage carefully in an airport.
6. You have to/must keep your head down when you hit a golf ball.
7. You have to/must carry your passport when you are traveling.
8. You have to/must practice English outside the classroom.
9. You have to/must listen to and respect your classmates.
10. You have to/must take the subway if you want to get around Tokyo quickly.

Exercise B *page 28*

2. Christine needed to practice Japanese more.
3. Dave and Mary had to see *Kabuki* before they left Japan.
4. Sachiko had to report to the office yesterday at 9:00 a.m.
5. Tetsuo and Akira needed to get hair cuts.
6. Hideo had to stay home with the children while Hiroko worked.
7. Toru had to exercise his shoulder every day.
8. Megumi and Hiroyuki didn't have to go to bed at 10 last night.
9. Mariko didn't have to call home last Wednesday.
10. You needed to drink a lot of water when you were climbing Mt. Fuji.

Exercise F *page 31*

2. What time will you have to be there tomorrow? (What time do you have to be there tomorrow?)
3. Do you have to study all night?
4. Yasuko won't have to wake up early next year.
5. What did she need to bring to the party?
6. Who has got to study with Paul tonight?
7. Nancy doesn't have to meet the president next week. (Nancy won't have to meet...)
8. They must pick up their aunt at the airport on Monday.
9. You had better buy your ticket fast if you want to get a good price.
10. Do Greg and Penny have to wait here all day?

Exercise G *page 32*

You must hurry up!
Mr. Vernon said we have to be in class by 10:30 today.
And we need to be ready for a big test.
I have to find a clean pair of jeans to wear, and I have to iron a blouse.
We have to get going or we'll be late.
You'd better forget about breakfast.
But I have to have a cup of coffee before I go...
Okay, but you've got to hurry.
You must use a pencil only and you need to check your work very carefully.
I have got to study more this semester.
The first thing I've got to do is get a decent grade on this test.
The second thing I need to do is get a stronger pair of glasses.

UNIT 5: PERMISSION/BRAZIL

Exercise A *(Possible Answers)* *page 35*

1. Can I play the piano?
   May I get something to drink?
   Could I see your stamp collection?

2. May I please look at the room?
   Could I see another room?
   May I use my credit card?

3. Could I check my bags now?
   May I change my seat assignment?
   Can I leave my bag with you?

4. Can I sit here?
   May I look at your paper?
   Could I ask a question?

5. May I pay with a credit card?
   Can I ask the price of this?
   Could I see another one?

6. Could I take a photograph in here?
   May I go outside and come back in?
   Can I ask you a question abut this painting.

7. Can I put this bag in the trunk?
   May I smoke in here?
   Could I pay with a twenty?

8. May I park near the science building?
   Can I get the assignment from you?
   Could I borrow your notes?

Exercise B *(Possible Answers)* *page 37*

1b. Could I return this shirt?
    Yes, you can.
    No, you can't.
1c. Can I go ahead of you?
    Yes, you can.
    No, you can't.

2a. May I take out this book?
    Yes, you can.
    No, you can't.

2b. Can I open the window?
Yes, you can.
No, you can't.
2c. Could I move this table and these chairs?
Yes, you can.
No, you can't.

3a. Can I park in your driveway?
Yes, you can.
No, you can't.
3b. Could we use your pool next week?
Yes, you can.
No, you can't.
3c. May I pick apples from your tree?
Yes, you can.
No, you can't.

Exercise C *(Possible Answers)* page 39

2. Can I use your CD player?
3. Could I borrow some money?
4. May I wear your blue jacket?
5. Can I use your telephone?
6. Could I try some of your cookies?
7. May I sit here?
8. Could I open the window?

Exercise D *page 40*

1. b
2. d
3. a
4. d
5. b
6. a
7. c

Exercise E *page 41*

2. May I borrow...?
3. Could we see...?
4. Can I go...?
5. Is he allowed to go...?
6. May we come...?
7. Can we use...?
8. Could I travel...?

Exercise F *page 42*

May I cut one or two of them to put on my table at home?
Can I have yours after you finish it?

A Possible List of Questions Mr. Johnson asked Daniel:
Could I use your bicycle?
Can I sit in your lawn chair and look at your garden?
May I borrow a cup of sugar?
Can I use your telephone?

UNIT 6: REQUEST/FRANCE

Exercise A *(Possible answers)* page 46

1. Can you bring me another cup of cafe au lait?
2. Would you mind taking me to the airport tomorrow?
3. Would you show me the best hotel in Brittany?
4. Could you tell me where the restrooms are?
5. Will you explain to me who built the Notre Dame Cathedral?
6. Can you carry my bags to that hotel near the Champs d'Elysees?
7. Would you mind lending me some money until I cash a traveler's check?
8. Could you open the window because it's very stuffy in here?

9. Can you give me a ride back to the station because I left my backpack there?
10. Would you write your address so I can send you a postcard from Strasbourg?

Exercise B (*Possible Answers*) *page 47*

1b. Could you give me an extra shopping bag?
Yes, I can.
No, I can't.
1c. Would you mind helping me carry my groceries?
No, I wouldn't.
Yes, I would.

2a. Can you show me how to use the computer?
Yes, I can.
No, I can't.
2b. Would you mind helping me find this book?
No, I wouldn't
Yes, I would.
2c. Could you speak a little more quietly?
Yes, we can.
No, we can't.

3a. Can you turn down the music?
Yes, we can.
No, we can't.
3b. Would you mind watering our plants?
No, we wouldn't.
Yes, we would.
3c. Will you help us move some furniture?
Yes, we will.
No, we won't.

Exercise D *page 49*

1. d   5. b
2. f   6. a
3. g   7. e
4. c

Exercise E *page 50*

And would you tell the cook to put lettuce on the side?
And could you tell the cook to use wheat bread?
Oh. And could you also ask him to toast the bread for me?
Could he put just a little mustard on the bread?
Would you bring me a glass of water now...?
Can you make my sandwich with Swiss cheese?
Could you make the sandwich with cheddar?
I'm sorry to bother you, but could you wrap this sandwich up for me?
Would you mind giving this to that nice waiter?

UNIT 7:   INVITATION/

UNITED ARAB EMERATES

Exercise A (*Possible Answers*) *page 54*

1. Can you study with me tonight?
Could you help me with my home work?
Shall we study together tonight?
2. Could you come to visit this weekend?
Would you like to come to my house?
Can you come to our house this week end?
3. Would you like to have dinner at the new Lebanese restaurant?
Do you want to have dinner at the Lebanese restaurant?
Would you have dinner with me at the Lebanese restaurant?
4. Would you like to go to a concert tonight?
Could you go with me to a concert?
Shall we go to a concert tonight?

5. Would you come to a party at my house?
   Would you like to come to a party this weekend?
   Could you come to our house for a party?
6. Could you go camel riding with us?
   Would you like to go camel riding?
   Would you go camel riding with us?

Exercise B (*Possible Answers*) *page 55*

2. Would you like to come for dinner?
3. Can you have lunch with me tomorrow?
4. Could you visit us this summer?
5. Can you come and watch me play basketball tomorrow night?
6. Could you go to the movies with me?

Exercise C (*Possible Answers*) *page 56*

2. Would you go to Khalaf's birthday party with me next weekend?
   Sure. That's a great idea.
   No, I wouldn't. I'm going out of town.
3. Would you like to go to a football game in Dubai?
   Yes, I'd like to.
   No, I'm sorry, but I have to work.
4. Can you have dinner on the restaurant boat tomorrow at 8?
   Yes, I can. That would be fun.
   No, I can't. Sorry.
5. Could you go hiking with me in Nepal next summer?
   Sure I could.
   No, I couldn't. I don't have a summer vacation.

Exercise D (*Possible Answers*) *page 57*

2. Can you play football with us today?
3. Would you like to go to the movies with me tonight?
4. Would you go golfing with me this afternoon?
5. Could you go camel riding with us?
6. Can you come to our party next week?
7. Would you like to go shopping tonight?
8. Can you come to the concert tomorrow?

Exercise E *page 58*

Would you like to come over for dinner on Friday night?
Could you come over on Thursday night instead?
Could we get together next week?

UNIT 8: DESIRE AND PREFERENCE /MALAYSIA

Exercise A (*Possible Answers*) *page 62*

France
   I would like to climb the Eiffel Tower.
Egypt
   I would like to see the Pyramids.
Japan
   I would like to climb Mt. Fuji.
Brazil
   I would like to go to Ipanema Beach.
Thailand
   I would like to go to Bangkok.
The United Arab Emirates
   I would like to go camping in the desert.

Exercise B (*Possible Answers*) *page 64*

France
1. Would you like to climb the Eiffel Tower?
2. Yes, I would.
3. No, I wouldn't.

Egypt
1. Would you like to see the Pyramids?
2. Yes, I would.
3. No, I wouldn't.

Japan
1. Would you like to climb Mt. Fuji?
2. Yes, I would.
3. No, I wouldn't.

Brazil
1. Would you like to go to Ipanema Beach?
2. Yes, I would.
3. No, I wouldn't.

Thailand
1. Would you like to go to Bangkok?
2. Yes, I would.
3. No, I wouldn't.

The United Arab Emirates
1. Would you like to go camping in the desert?
2. Yes, I would.
3. No, I wouldn't.

Exercise C (*Possible Answers*) *page 66*

2. I'd rather watch TV.
3. I'd rather study English in Australia.
4. I'd rather eat chocolate ice cream.
5. I'd prefer to eat dinner at home.
6. I'd rather go to bed early and get up early.
7. I'd rather travel by boat.
8. I'd prefer to live in the city.
9. I'd prefer to spend my vacation at the beach.

Exercise D (*Possible Answers*) *page 67*

2. Would you rather watch a video or go to the cinema?
   Would you prefer to watch a video or go to the cinema?
3. Would you rather go to a museum or visit an art gallery?
   Would you prefer to go to a museum or visit an art gallery?
4. Would you rather drive a car or ride a bicycle?

Would you prefer to drive a car or ride a bicycle?
5. Would you rather live in Paris or New York?
   Would you prefer to live in Paris or New York?
6. Would you rather go swimming or go jogging on the beach?
   Would you prefer to go swimming or go jogging on the beach?
7. Would you rather study French or study Italian?
   Would you prefer to study French or study Italian?

Exercise E (*Possible Answers*) *page 68*

2. I would have preferred to watch...
3. She would sooner have visited...
4. They wouldn't have liked to live...
5. Jean and George would have rather stayed in a hotel...
6. She wanted to see...
7. We'd have preferred to go...
8. Sylvie would have liked to meet us...
9. I'd have preferred to take...
10. We wanted to learn a little Malay...

Exercise F *page 69*

I want to go with you.
I don't want to stay home.
I want Cocoa Snacks for breakfast.
I would like to buy a few vegetables and some bananas.
But I want Cocoa Snacks for breakfast!
Thomas, would you rather have spinach or broccoli for dinner tonight?
Ma, I want some of these chocolate bars.
Would you prefer apples or bananas?
I don't want apples or bananas.
I want chocolate.
I'd rather have bananas for dessert.
I want to play video games before we go home.

UNIT 9: FUTURE AND WILLINGNESS/CHINA

Exercise A *page 73*

2. You are going to...
   Phil and I are going to...
3. Wudi isn't going to...
   I'm not going to...
4. Leslie is going to...
   Johnny and Ling are going to...
5. What is Zhu going to do tomorrow?
   What are Lee and Meng going to do tomorrow?

Exercise B *page 74*

2. What will Yumiko and Hussein remember?
   Yumiko and Hussein won't remember their class in the USA.
3. What will Ji help you clean?
   Ji won't help you clean your apartment.
4. Where will Lina and Shirley work after they finish school?
   Lina and Shirley won't work in Hong Kong after they finish school.
5. When will my friend finish the Chinese cooking class?
   My friend won't finish the Chinese cooking class in two months.
6. What time will Ting and Eng begin their golf match?
   Ting and Eng won't begin their golf match at 12 noon.

Exercise D *page 76*

1. Willingness
2. Plan
3. Prediction
4. Prediction
5. Willingness
6. Expectation
7. Immediate Future
8. Plan
9. Prediction
10. Willingness

Exercise E *page 77*

2. are you going to
   going to
   will
   will
   am going to/will
3. will
   will

Exercise F *page 78*

I'm going to fly direct from Chicago to Hong Kong on January 5.
...I'll be on the plane for about 15 hours.
I won't stay overnight there.
I'm not going to bring too much money, ...
...I won't spend what little I have in Hong Kong.
...I'll transfer to a direct flight to Hebei.
...I won't even know I'm flying.
Will you meet me at the airport in Hebei?
This will be my first trip anywhere.
Speaking a few words of Chinese will be strange.
I'll bring the clothes you want.
Mom says she's going to make you another sweater.
...I'll probably bring that, too.
I'm not going to leave for a few more weeks...
I'll see you next month.

UNIT 10: POSSIBILITY/INDIA

Exercise A *page 81*

2. She may (might/could) go swimming.
3. He may (might, could) be finished with the exam by now.
4. Radeesh may not (might not) have enough money to visit Calcutta.
5. Manoj may (might, could) want to eat vadai for breakfast.
6. She may (might, could) call next week.
7. Diane may not (might not) know when Ismail will return from his trip to Jaipur.
8. They may not (might not) stay in the Maharaja's palace in Udaipur because it's expensive.
9. Raju and Mona may (might, could) be too tired to walk to the Red Fort.
10. Frances and Antonio may not (might not) be going to Agra tomorrow.

Exercise B *page 82*

1. It may (might, could) have rained ...
2. She may (might/could) have gone to the temples...
3. He may (might, could) have been finished with the exam ...
4. Radeesh may not (might not) have had enough time to visit Calcutta.
5. Manoj may (might, could) have wanted to eat vadai for breakfast.
6. She may (might, could) have called...
7. Diane may not (might not) have known when Ismail would return from his trip to Jaipur.
8. We may not (might not) have stayed in the Maharaja's palace in Udaipur because it's expensive.
9. Raju and Mona may (might, could) have been too tired to walk to the Red Fort.
10. Frances and Antonio may not (might not) have gone to Agra.

Exercise F *page 87*

2. Ajay looks sick because he may have gotten too much sun.
3. Sridevi might not have gone too far from home because her car is in the driveway.
4. The accident may have been caused when the blue car went through the red light.
5. Ravi could want to watch a baseball game when he comes to visit.
   When Ravi comes to visit, he could want to watch a baseball game.

Exercise G *page 88*

Examples from the story:
   It might rain.
   Anita was thinking how she might get him out of bed without going upstairs...
   Ashok may have heard the noise, but he didn't come downstairs.
   He may not have heard the vacuum...
   ...but this could be the thing to get him out of bed.
   The vacuum might not have bothered him.

UNIT 11: PROBABILITY/MEXICO

Exercise A *page 92*

1. should/ought to
2. should/ought to
3. should/ought to
4. should/ought to
5. should/ought to

Exercise B *page 92*
1. can't/couldn't
2. must/has to/has got to
3. can't/couldn't
4. must/have to/have got to
5. must

Exercise C *page 93*

1. must/has to
   should/ought to
2. must/have to
   should/ought to
3. should/ought to
   should/ought to/must
4. should/ought to
   must/have to
5. should/ought to
   must
6. should/ought to
   must
7. should/ought to
   must

Exercise D *page 94*

2. Patricio can't have been in Hermosillo. He didn't have a reservation until...
3. Alejandra and MarÌa ought to have been at the party tonight because they love to dance...
4. He must not have liked me very much. He never called.
5. My brother couldn't have been in Monterrey. He lives 1,000 miles from there.

6. You can't have been serious when you said that you were leaving me forever.

Exercise E *page 94*

1. This letter has to be from my friend in Thailand.
2. The doctor ought to be in his office now.
3. I should have time to visit you next summer.
4. The students must not have studied for the exam.
5. My sister couldn't have been at the conference in Japan.

Exercise G *page 96*

2. shouldn't/ought not to
3. can't/couldn't
4. must have/had to have
5. should/ought to
6. couldn't have/can't have
7. couldn't have/can't have
8. must not have
9. should/ought to
10. must/has to

Exercise H *page 97*

She couldn't have gone out without calling me or leaving me a note.
Something must have happened to her.
No, she couldn't have had something else to do.
Something serious had to have happened to her.
She should be home by now. She ought to be there, but she isn't.
I told you she ought to be there, but she isn't.
Something terrible had to have happened to her.
I must be overtired or something to be reacting like this.
I just have this feeling that something bad must have happened.

UNIT 12: PAST HABITUAL ACTIONS/GERMANY

Exercise A *page 101*

1. e   6. h
2. i   7. j
3. f   8. b
4. c   9. d
5. a   10. g

Exercise B *page 101*

2. used to/would
3. used to/would
   used to/would
4. used to
   used to/would (would is better)
5. used to/would
6. used to/would
7. used to
   used to/would

Exercise C *page 102*

2. When did the Hoeferts use to eat a big meal?
   Did the Hoeferts use to eat a big meal every evening?
   The Hoeferts didn't use to eat a big meal every evening.
3. What did Franz use to wear?
   Did Franz use to wear glasses?
   Franz didn't use to wear glasses.
4. When would your mother, your sister and you get up?
   Would your mother, your sister and you get up at six and walk in the park?
   Your mother, your sister and you wouldn't get up at six and walk in the park.
5. Where did Reggie use to go skiing?
   Did Reggie use to go skiing in the Alps?
   Reggie didn't use to go skiing in the Alps.

6. What would you and Christina do every Tuesday night?
   Would you and Christina hike every Tuesday night?
   Christina and you wouldn't hike every night.
7. When did students use to do their presentations?
   Did students use to do their presentations on the last day of class?
   Students didn't use to do their presentations on the last day of class.
8. Who used to be good friends before they got married and divorced?
   Did Art and Clara use to be good friends before they got married and divorced?
   Art and Clara didn't use to be good friends before they got married and divorced.

Exercise F *page 107*

I often think about how things used to be.
...but I really do enjoy remembering all the things I used to do when I was a young man.
I would always get up before the sun because there was always so much to do.
We lived on a farm, and I would milk the cows, clean the barn and feed the chickens before breakfast.
I used to love the way the sunlight sparkled on the fields.
Now, there are houses and condominiums where all those fields used to be.
I used to stand quietly and listen to the birds chirping in the trees...
I would listen for the roosters and my neighbors on the other farms.
We all would get up at about the same time and do pretty much the same things.
When I heard the church bells strike 6:00, I would go inside the house, wash up and have a big breakfast.

She used to make me pancakes and eggs and fresh coffee, but she wouldn't eat with me.

She would only watch me and my father and brothers and make sure we had everything we needed.

After lunch I would work outdoors until lunchtime.

I used to be so happy when Ma finally called us in to eat.

I would work so hard that I had the appetite of two men.

We would work long and hard hours, and we lived a very simple life.

My cousins from the city used to visit, and I remember thinking that I might like to live there one day.

I would dream about leaving the farm, but I never did.

I used to think about what life would be like if I could get away.

I used to wonder about all the things I might do. Now, that future has come and gone.

... that boy in the field listening to the roosters and birds used to imagine that...

UNIT 13: DIRECT AND INDIRECT SPEECH/TURKEY

Exercise A *page 111*

1. Jeannie said she couldn't believe how beautiful Bolu was in the autumn.
2. Hisham said that they shouldn't wait too long to buy their World Cup tickets.
3. Burak said that I mustn't call home too many times or I would get home sick.
4. Nancy said that I had to remember not to miss our trip to the Blue Mosque.
5. Mrs. Hamilton told the waiter that she would have another cup of Turkish coffee.

6. Nihal said that Carrie and Alexandra were going to Erzurum on Monday.
7. Bill told Nuri that he would see him in September.
8. Hülya told me that Ayla had to call her this weekend.
9. Phil said that Edgar might stop in Edirne on his way to Greece.
10. He told his wife that she had to be crazy if she thought he wanted to spend the holiday with her family.

Exercise B *page 112*

1. Jeannie asked Aydin what time she would leave tomorrow.
2. Hisham asked Ahmed why he had to go to Gallipolli alone.
3. John asked me if he should visit the Tetrapylon when he's in Aphrodisias.
4. Sevim asked Nancy if she would like to go to a taverna.

5. Jeremy asked Toru if he was going to go to Capadocia.
6. Bruce asked where I would stay in Bursa.
7. Bill asked Heidi if she could speak Turkish.
8. Paulina asked Deniz where she should eat when she visited Izmir.

9. Ray asked us if we wanted to go to Bodrum with him.
10. Khamees and Abdulla asked if they had to carry their passports in Turkey.

The Colosseum

UNIT 14: CONDITIONALS/ITALY

Exercise A *(Possible Answers)* *page 114*

1. ...he won't be able to enjoy traveling in Italy.
2. ...you should visit Agrigento.
3. ...she has to find a sponsor.
4. ...I'll call my parents at home.
5. ...I must be crazy because I'm not a good driver.
6. ...they will miss one of the most beautiful cities in the world.
7. ...he had better come back again.
8. ...we have to take a lot of pictures.
9. ...they can (will be able to) save a lot of money.
10. ...you mustn't stay in your hotel.

Exercise B *(Possible Answers)* *page 115*

1. ...I would eat a lot of good food.
2. ...he could learn about the great Italian painters and sculptors.
3. ...she might meet many interesting people.

4. ...they might have had to spend another week in Italy.
5. ...they could have traveled around a lot more easily.
6. ...I would call the embassy right away.
7. ...they might not have seen any Greek ruins.
8. ...she could go to almost any restaurant in Italy.
9. ...I would spend more time in Florence.
10. ...I could have stayed longer in St. Peter's Basilica.

Exercise C *(Example sentences only)* *page 116*

1. If I finish..., I can go...
2. If Myra had gotten up..., she would have seen...
3. If we came..., we might get...
4. If Zeinab studied..., she could do...
5. If Evan works..., he will learn...
6. If Dan wants to play..., he has to practice...
7. If you are hungry..., you mustn't order...
8. If Lamia hadn't gone..., she couldn't have learned...
9. If Youssef cooked more..., he could save...
10. If I talk to myself, I must be going crazy.

Other books from Pro Lingua
AT THE INTERMEDIATE-ADVANCED LEVEL

Solo, Duo, Trio — Puzzles and games for individual students or small groups. Builds vocabulary; photocopyable for handouts.

Shenanigames — Grammar-focused, interactive ESL activities and games providing practice with a full range of grammar structures. Photocopyable.

Getting a Fix on Vocabulary — A student text and workbook that focuses on affixation— building words by adding prefixes and suffixes to a root.

Lexicarry — Pictures for Learning Languages the Active Way. Over 4500 everyday words and expressions in 192 contexts that make conversation and interactive learning easy. There is a special new section on proverbs and sayings. Lots of words, even for very advanced students. Additional material at www.Lexicarry.com.

Stranger in Town — A dramatic radio play in which the stranger moving to a small town is a metaphor for the process of cultural adjustment. Tapescript book and tape.

Nobel Prize Winners — 18 brief biographies for listening and/or reading. All the reading passages are also available as gapped exercises for reading or dictation. Text and three cassettes.

Discussion Strategies — Carefully structured pair and small group work. Excellent preparation for students who will participate in academic or professional work that requires effective participation in discussion and seminars.

Write for You — A teacher resource book with copyable handouts. The focus is on creative activities that lead to effective writing by intermediate students who are intending to further their education.

People at Work — An integrated skills program that centers on recorded interviews with 10 real working people — intern, engineeer, contractor, educator, small business owner, and others. One text, one teacher's guide, and three cassettes.

Pearls of Wisdom — At the heart of this integrated skills builder are twelve stories from Africa and the Caribbean, collected and told by Dr. Raouf Mama of Benin. Student text for reading/listening, workbook for discussion/vocabulary building, two cassettes.

Web Store: www.ProLinguaAssociates.com